FREEDOM FROM RELIGION

FREEDOM FROM RELIGION

RIGHTS AND NATIONAL SECURITY

Amos N. Guiora

OXFORD
UNIVERSITY PRESS

OXFORD

UNIVERSITY PRESS

*Oxford University Press, Inc., publishes works that further Oxford University's
objective of excellence in research, scholarship, and education.*

Copyright © 2009 by Oxford University Press, Inc.
Published by Oxford University Press, Inc.
198 Madison Avenue, New York, New York 10016

Oxford is a registered trademark of Oxford University Press
Oxford University Press is a registered trademark of
Oxford University Press, Inc.

Library of Congress Cataloging-in-Publication Data

Guiora, Amos N., 1957-
Freedom from religion : rights and national security / Amos N. Guiora.
p. cm.
Includes bibliographical references and index.
ISBN 978-0-19-538925-8 ((hardback) : alk. paper)
1. Freedom of religion. 2. Freedom of religion—United States.
I. Title.
K3258.G85 2009
342.08'52—dc22   2009019132

1 2 3 4 5 6 7 8 9
Printed in the United States of America on acid-free paper

Note to Readers:

This publication is designed to provide accurate and authoritative information in regard to the
subject matter covered. It is based upon sources believed to be accurate and reliable and is intended
to be current as of the time it was written. It is sold with the understanding that the publisher is not
engaged in rendering legal, accounting, or other professional services. If legal advice or other expert
assistance is required, the services of a competent professional person should be sought. Also, to
confirm that the information has not been affected or changed by recent developments, traditional
legal research techniques should be used, including checking primary sources where appropriate.

*(Based on the Declaration of Principles jointly adopted by a Committee of the
American Bar Association and a Committee of Publishers and Associations.)*

> **You may order this or any other Oxford University Press publication
> by visiting the Oxford University Press website at www.oup.com**

To the Rev. Dr. John C. Lentz, Jr. A truer friend one could not hope for. His sage advice, extraordinary humor, and honest criticism made this book possible.

To Anne Frank. Her diary, written in an age of unimaginable horror, represents the honesty and hope of young people everywhere.

To Sandra Samuel, an Indian nanny who—in the face of immediate death by religious extremists bent on killing innocent men, women, and children—saved a young boy, thereby representing the best of the human spirit.

TABLE OF CONTENTS

PREFACE

"That as religion, or the duty which we owe to our divine and omnipotent Creator, and the manner of discharging it, can be governed only by reason and conviction, not by force or violence; and therefore that *all men should enjoy the fullest toleration in the exercise of religion,* according to the dictates of conscience, unpunished and unrestrained by the Magistrates, unless, **under color of religion, any man disturb the peace, the happiness, or safety of society, or of individuals**. And that it is the mutual duty of all to practice Christian forbearance, love and charity towards each other."

Virginia Declaration of Rights—
a forerunner to the Declaration of Independence,
George Mason's version of Article XVI

I am not a religious person, so how do I allow myself the privilege, perhaps arrogance, of writing a book about religion? That is, how can someone not steeped in the intricacies of any particular faith write a book about religion, much less about the *limits* of religion, entitling it "Freedom from Religion"? To this significant question I offer the following response: while I am not an expert on religion, my entire professional career has been spent trying to understand the role of religion as the primary motivator for one of the greatest threats facing civil society today—terrorism.

I have been asked on countless occasions why I chose to write this book; my answer is unequivocal. As the only child of two Holocaust survivors, I well understand the price of passivity.

The essential assumption of this book is that religion is central to the human existence. While not always understandable, the reality is best summed up as "it is what it is." Whether religion holds society together or comforts people in times of personal stress or eases fears associated with death, it is an undeniable reality in the lives of hundreds of millions of people worldwide.

While defining religion is no mean task, the thesis explored in this book does not address all aspects of religion. Rather, the focus is on *religious extremism*—the greatest danger faced by the liberal state today. What limits, if any, are placed on religious extremism is the essence of our focus. The question of whether limits need be placed on religious practice is premised on a belief that domestic public order and national security require addressing this issue, candidly and truthfully.

The emphasis of this inquiry is not theological in orientation. Rather it is focused on national security and public order. Perhaps in a different age the questions would address various political regimes and movements, ranging from the far right to the far left. But, that is not the case, for the main danger to contemporary liberal, democratic society no longer comes from secular extremism, but from religious extremism. The fundamental premise of this book is to ask *how* a liberal society protects itself against religious extremism, and proposing concrete recommendations for implementing protective measures.

During the course of my twenty-year career in the Judge Advocate General's Corps of the Israel Defense Forces, I was significantly involved in the legal and policy aspects of operational counterterrorism. Commensurate with that professional experience, I developed a deep understanding and respect for the absolute requirement to balance legitimate, individual civil rights with equally legitimate national security considerations.

In the context of the contemporary era of terrorism, there is no choice *but* to discuss religion and its practice. A primary motivation for numerous terrorist organizations world-wide (whether region-specific or global) is religion. Understanding religion as a motivator is essential to understanding terrorism, and therefore counter-terrorism.

That reality—terror in the name of God—is *the* reality of our current milieu. It may well be the reality for our children and grandchildren. Precisely because of that, we must have a mature, frank and candid discussion regarding religion. That discussion is not, under any circumstances, America-centric; quite the opposite is true. Societies worldwide are under attack in the name of God.

I have decided that in order to make my case as compelling and convincing as possible I must look "the tiger in the eye." Otherwise, I will be joining a long list of authors who have shied away from directly addressing the extraordinary danger religious extremism poses to society.

Writing a book about religion, or more accurately, about limiting religion, is a journey into unfamiliar territory for a secularist. It has only been possible to do so because people from all walks of life have come forward and agreed to share their opinions, perspectives, scholarship, and beliefs with me. As I repeatedly told colleagues and friends, I was literally overwhelmed with how many people were willing to meet with me. In the five countries under study I have communicated with hundreds of people, who freely gave of their time, talent, experience and wisdom.

To all, I am most grateful for educating me in the intricacies of your faith, religion, and field of expertise. You were generous, candid and critical; you have my unending respect, thanks and gratitude. That said, I would be remiss were I not to acknowledge in particular the friendship, forthrightness and wonderful collegiality of Prof. Leslie Francis, Prof. Terry Kogan, Prof. David Little, Prof. Scott Matheson, the Honorable Judge Michael McConnell, Dean Martha Minow, and Prof. Tom Zwart.

My designation as a Fulbright Senior Specialist at the University of Utrecht was instrumental in facilitating my understanding of the Netherlands as it afforded me the opportunity to engage with Dutch colleagues and officials.

While all mistakes are mine, I have been the beneficiary of an extraordinary team of research assistants. The hours and energy invested by RuthAnne Frost, Brady Stuart and Artemis Vamianakis —all class of '09, SJ Quinney College of Law, the University of Utah—have truly humbled me. These recent graduates have, collectively and individually, challenged and argued with me every step of the way. Without a doubt, both the reader and I are the better for their commitment to this project. I can but stand and applaud. The reader will note that the appendix carries their names—this is not by chance, as they approached me and asked if they could write it. I immediately said 'yes', as did Oxford University Press. RuthAnne, Brady and Artemis deserve the recognition and credit.

My Dean and good friend, Hiram Chodosh, has been an extraordinary supporter of this project—both in terms of generously making resources available and by providing the moral support so necessary for a project of this nature. I am, as always, most grateful to Hiram for creating a unique research and writing environment at the SJ Quinney College of Law. My colleagues and I are the beneficiaries of his tremendous efforts.

Kevin Pendergast, my editor at OUP, has been involved in the book every step of the way as he graciously agreed to read and comment on the draft of each chapter. His comments have been forthright, candid and spot-on. For that, I am most grateful.

I also send a warm word of thanks to my friends at the Starbucks in Sugarhouse, Salt Lake City, for their constant encouragement and interest.

Finally, to the reader—this book is not an 'easy read'; nor is it intended to be. I can but hope you will find it thought-provoking and view it for what it is intended to be—a clarion call for action.

CHAPTER ONE

IGNORING THE STORM

December 17, 2008 – December 20, 2008

London, England

"The multitudes remained plunged in ignorance of the simplest economic facts, and their leaders, seeking their votes, did not dare to undeceive them. The newspapers, after their fashion, reflected and emphasized the prevailing opinions."

– Winston Churchill, *The Gathering Storm*

In December 2008, I met with politicians, security officials, and academics in the United Kingdom to get a British perspective on what I consider to be the greatest threat to civil society that this generation will face—religious extremism. It was an experience that profoundly impacted the fundamental thesis of this book.

When I first conceived of writing a book about the threat of religious extremism, I planned to examine and analyze legal and policy issues relevant to the five countries: the United States, the United Kingdom, the Netherlands, Turkey, and Israel. The book's chapters would be formed around a specific topic—the limits of freedom of speech, separation of church and state, the free exercise of religion—and the five countries would hopefully provide context and insight about religious extremism in the modern age. While I expected to concentrate most heavily on the United States and Israel—the two countries in which I live and have citizenship—I thought that complete chapters on individual countries would be unnecessary for my purposes. It was only after visiting the UK that I decided to change this plan.

The day of my arrival, the banner headline in every major newspaper throughout the UK was that those responsible for the 2007 Glasgow International Airport terrorist attacks had been convicted of their crimes. On that day, my loquacious cab driver shared his worldview with me, ultimately concluding, "Why can't Muslims just be like us?" I had no doubt that his sentiments were not unique among the British populace.

As I made my way to a meeting with a senior security official in London— who, after greeting me graciously, began our conversation with the words,

"Professor Guiora, it is the government's position that Islam is a religion of peace"—the Home Affairs Minister of the Netherlands reported an increase in the number of Islamic extremists in the Netherlands. This juxtaposition of opinions from across the North Sea would highlight the difference between the United Kingdom and the other four countries examined in this book.

While a cab driver in London felt comfortable expressing somewhat prejudiced sentiments in front of a stranger, the majority of British law-makers and academics with whom I met expressed extraordinary caution in addressing religious extremism. I began my trip to the UK under the impression that the British experience in Northern Ireland—referred to as "The Troubles"—would leave Britons less prone to political correct-ness. I ended the trip with the troubling impression that British lawmak-ers were deliberately ignoring a serious problem confronting not only their own country, but democracies around the globe.

Twenty-eight percent of British Muslims believe that British authorities "go over the top in trying not to offend Muslims."[1] It is not hard to see where such an opinion comes from. After the July 7, 2005 subway bomb-ings, Scotland Yard Deputy Assistant Commissioner Brian Paddick declared, "'Islamic' and 'terrorist' are two words that do not go together."[2] While Paddick's obvious intent was to prevent public outrage against innocent Muslims, the fact is, his statement was flatly wrong. Of course not all Muslims living in the UK are terrorists—it would take a truly obtuse individual to leap to that conclusion—but the undeniable fact is that all the recent terrorist attacks in the United Kingdom, as distinct from Northern Ireland, have been committed by British Muslims. Is it so difficult to acknowledge an evident truth?

For one reason or another, the British government is not willing to acknowledge the reality of religious extremism in its country, and is often willing to go to great lengths to paint the problem in a different light. For example, one member of the Labour Party with whom I spoke insisted that the root cause of radicalization was not religion, but socio-economic status. Facts suggest a different story. As has been previously

---

1   *British Muslims poll: Key Points*, BBC ONLINE, January 29, 2007, *available at* http://news.bbc.co.uk/2/hi/uk_news/6309983.stm

2   Steve Doughty, *Threat of up to Two Million Muslim Terrorists, Warns Community Leader*, September 11, 2006, *available at* http://www.dailymail.co.uk/news/article-404525/Threat-million-Muslim-terrorists-warns-community-leader.html

FREEDOM FROM RELIGION

documented, the 19 hijackers involved in 9/11 came from middle- to upper-class backgrounds.[3] Most of them were highly educated. Similarly, the most recent terror attacks in Great Britain (three completed, one thwarted) have been carried out by British citizens from middle- and upper-class backgrounds. These facts belie socioeconomic arguments, leaving religion to explain the actions of these few extremists.

The attitude of an unwillingness to lay blame is similarly reflected in the British media. During the November 2008 terrorist attacks in Mumbai, the BBC and other UK media insisted on referring to the terrorist responsible for killing 101 people as "gunmen." One report even added the adjective "youthful" to gunmen, as if their age excused their behavior.

I shared my puzzlement over this phenomenon with a British academic whose response was helpful. "Looking the tiger in the eye," as I had put it, "would necessitate an acknowledgment that the tiger even exists." This, apparently, is presently unacceptable to the British government.

Some of the individuals I spoke to went even further, claiming that the true danger to the United Kingdom was not the threat posed by religious extremists, but the potential harm to British society that would result were the government to emphasize the Islamic nature of religious terrorism. Contemporary British society is extraordinarily multicultural. London alone boasts a population that speaks over 300 different languages and 50 non-indigenous communities, each with a population of more than 10,000.[4]

The majority of recent British terrorists were of Pakistani origin, Islamic by birth; others were converts to Islam.[5] Whether new converts or Islamic by birth, the reality is, frankly, indisputable. Furthermore, British Prime Minister Gordon Brown has suggested that three quarters of the gravest terror plots under investigation in the United Kingdom

---

3   For a greater discussion of the 9/11 hijackers, see Terry McDermott's book, *Perfect Soldiers.*

4   *Available at* http://www.guardian.co.uk/uk/2005/jan/21/britishidentity1.

5   Including Nicky Reilly, who is considered the first "one person" suicide bomber cell who was injured when the bomb he had prepared exploded. Reilly (Saeed Alim) was a recent convert to Islam, http://www.timesonline.co.uk/tol/news/uk/crime/article3985830.ece

had links to Pakistan.[6] If the plots had links to Pakistan, then it is a safe bet they also had links to extremists in the Pakistani community in the United Kingdom.

Stating the truth is not an indictment of all Muslims. Avoiding the truth reflects an institutionalized resistance to acknowledging the elephant in the room. However, the British government's desire to avoid references to theories espoused in books such as *Londonistan*[7] and *While Europe Slept*[8] is obvious.

This hesitation is no doubt impacted by Britain's imperial past. The sense of historic guilt over being a former colonial power was on the tip of numerous tongues during conversations in London. Even those willing to acknowledge the dangers inherent in extremist religion proposed that the appropriate response would not involve government agencies. While British law enforcement advocates the power to act proactively, the government's emphasis continues to be on prevention[9] via community outreach. It was suggested time and time again that change in the Islamic community must come from within, moderates engaging extremists.

Ultimately, the logic behind this proposal is extremely problematic. Regardless of whether British politicians are willing to acknowledge the threat of extremist religions, it is frankly unclear what role extremist imams[10] play in the radicalization of Muslims in England. Many British policymakers and academics believe that extreme Muslims in the United

---

6   *Available at* http://www.timesonline.co.uk/tol/news/uk/article5339975.ece, last visited December 20, 2008

7   *Londonistan: How Britain is Creating a Terror State Within* by Melanie Phillips, a best-seller published in 2006, argues that weak policing, cultural relativism, and "victim culture" in London contribute to an ideal breeding ground for Islamic terrorists.

8   *While Europe Slept: How Radical Islam is Destroying the West from Within* by Bruce Bawer argues that Europe's cities are plagued with "radical Islam," which has provoked honor killings, political assassinations, the Madrid subway bombing, and the massacre of school children at Beslan. Bawer argues that radical Islamism is an equal threat to Nazism.

9   Prevention is one of the four "P's" of England's counter-radicalization policy, along with protection, preparation and pursuit. *See* http://security.homeoffice.gov.uk/counter-terrorism-strategy/about-the-strategy/

10   *See* Trial of Abu Hamza al-Masri, http://news.bbc.co.uk/1/hi/uk/4690224.stm, last visited December 21, 2008.

Kingdom are engaged in self-radicalization, rather than acting on religious incitement articulated by imams. While other governments understand with whom they are dealing—Fundamentalist Latter Day Saints Church leaders in the United States, rabbis in the West Bank, imams in the Netherlands—the British government is facing a more grassroots movement. During much of my visit, I was constantly reminded that Islam is not a hierarchal religion—"There is no Pope" was a recurring refrain.

This makes any limits on religious freedoms that might be applicable in the Israeli, Dutch, Turkish, or American paradigms difficult to apply in a British context. I came to the UK with the basic belief that when individuals with religious authority speak, they should be held to a higher standard of responsibility for their words. After all, religious extremism is largely cleric dependent. The impetus for religious extremism based action is dependent on an extremist interpretation of scripture or faith, as defined by an authority figure.

In the United Kingdom model, we are presented with uncertainty as to who is responsible from an authority perspective, which consequently leads to ambiguity regarding whose religious speech and conduct should potentially be limited. To that end, the difficulties expressed by experts regarding possible limitations are apparently warranted. If religious extremists in the UK are indeed self-radicalized, then security officials, policy analysts, and, ultimately, government leaders are hard-pressed to determine whose religious speech or conduct should be limited.

First-generation immigrants to the UK came from South Asia, North Africa, and English-speaking Caribbean nations. While these immigrants were expected to perform largely menial tasks, their intention was to stay in Britain and provide their children with a brighter future. To that end, they sought to provide their children with British educational opportunities in the hope that they would become "British." In sending their children to university, first generation immigrants did not expect that many would become radicalized. That is, rather than further integrating and assimilating into British society, many second- and third-generation immigrants have chosen to turn inwards to their communities and become newly religious at the expense of their parents' dream.

While the British government suggests that moderates will win an ideological fight, certain questions remain. Why would the extremists listen to the moderates? Why would the moderates ever volunteer for such a job? I do not mean to demean the idea of community outreach, and think it has an important role to play in any state's strategy regarding extreme groups. I mean to merely point out that a government's actions cannot be limited to delegating the responsibility of protecting society from extremism to society itself. After all, why else do we have a government, if not to protect us from internal and external threats alike?

This book ultimately proposes actions that governments could and should take in responding to religious extremism. When I presented of some the ideas that will be described in greater detail in subsequent chapters—broadening the definition of incitement, for example—they were rejected outright by my British audience. While these theories have not been met with universal acclaim—some American colleagues expressed concern with certain premises and disagreed with my conclusions—the level of political correctness in my British meetings was qualitatively different. In one meeting, an extremely thoughtful academic literally refused to use the phrase "religious extremism," except to suggest that I ought not to use the term.

The political realities in the UK prevent the adoption of what I recommend in this book—re-articulation of free speech and free exercise limitations. Elsewhere in this book, I am critical both of Israeli law enforcement officials and the judicial community for insufficiently responding to the clear threat posed by Jewish extremist settlers in the West Bank. In the same vein, I suggest that American authorities should have acted more forcefully, and sooner, to protect underage girls from harm in their FLDS communities.

While these criticisms may also apply to the United Kingdom, the overwhelming impression is of a society in a state of denial regarding the threat of religious extremism. This prevents potential remedies from even being considered. In this sense, the discussion regarding religious extremism in England is less legal, more policy.

Accordingly, the London of December 2008 is an appropriate place to begin this discussion, for the United Kingdom represents the greatest danger of all—ignoring reality. There must be a major philosophical change in how religious extremism is addressed by all policymakers, not just British ones. The United Kingdom is our baseline. On December 18, 2008—the day after I arrived in Great Britain, one day after every major daily newspaper was emblazoned with headlines of convicted terrorists—all the newspapers in London 'moved on' to a new event.

Religious extremism presents an extraordinary threat to democracies today. As such, we cannot afford to 'move on' until we have soberly discussed concrete recommendations for how governments and societies are to confront this reality while respecting the individual liberties of people of faith and protecting public order and security.

CHAPTER TWO

THE THREAT OF RELIGIOUS EXTREMISM

INTRODUCTION

Freedom of conscience is arguably the most important aspect of a democratic society. This freedom includes freedom of thought, speech, and religious conduct. Such freedom, exercised by individuals within a larger society, can result in positive progression of a society (abolitionists, women suffragists, civil rights activists) but also in movements that would destroy the very freedom that allowed them to exist in the first place (fascists and communists).

Within this larger freedom is freedom of religion. Religion is a powerful motivator for both positive social change and mass violence. It is an institution that is protected in civil society, whether by a nation's own constitution, domestic law, or international agreement. It is also a force in society that is difficult for many with a secular mindset to truly understand. When religion is promoting the positive development of society, it is an institution that is tolerated or even celebrated. When religion is tearing down the fabric of society, however, it is rarely condemned in any meaningful way. Democratic governments tend to shy away from curtailing civil rights, particularly the freedom of religion. Drawing the line between potentially questionable practices and those which truly endanger society is a difficult task; many democracies ignore the challenge.

Yet contemporary societies must begin to draw the line and take effective action against that which falls on the wrong side. Religious-based violence is a threat to democratic society on several levels. Religion is used as a motivator to commit wide-scale acts of terrorism, to justify individual acts of violence behind closed doors, and promote hatred of the "other." Given that religious violence constitutes such a grave threat to democracies, governments must begin to examine this institution more critically than in the past.

This book discusses the framework that modern democratic governments should adopt if they are to both protect the freedom of religion and effectively respond to a unique threat to safety. The primary thesis of this book is that civil societies cannot afford to continue to treat religion as an "untouchable" subject. We must begin to understand what religious extremism is and then to determine when and how it may be limited for the benefit of larger society.

DEFINING EXTREMIST RELIGION

What is religion? Many have commented, written, spoken, and pontificated on this question, and it would appear that the answer is relative for it depends on one's particular perspective, milieu, and culture. However, precision and conciseness is critical. After all, how can we limit something if we do not fully know what it is?

According to the Rev. Dr. John C. Lentz Jr., religion cannot be viewed in a vacuum; it is part of something else. It is cultural, internal, and related to an individual's ethics and ethnicity. It is always part of something larger. For hundreds upon hundreds of millions of people worldwide—from time immemorial—religion has been the essence of their existence. For people of faith, religion—*however it is to be defined*—is at the core of who they are.

Conversely, for non-believers—whether agnostics, atheists, or those disaffected from a particular faith—religion can be a source of many emotions ranging from skepticism to fear to suspended disbelief. Whether we view the definition of religion as "descriptive" (*what do people identify as religion?*) or "normative" (*what counts as a "religion"?*), there is no one clear definition of religion. That theme is critical to this book—your religion is whatever you determine it to be; your faith is your faith and therefore religion will *not* be defined. It is, in many ways, indefinable and depends on a personal interpretation of the relationship between an individual and his or her God.

Because our primary focus is on the confluence between religious *extremism* and national security, it is imperative that extremism be defined, even if religion itself cannot be. Religious extremism is when the actor believes that his or her tenets and principles are infallible and that *any* action, even violence, taken on behalf of those beliefs is justified. The action can be directed both at people of other faiths (or those of no faith), as well as members of the same religion who have violated the extremist's understanding of how their religion is to be practiced. Religious extremism is fundamentally and existentially different from secular terrorism for it lays claim to acting in the name of the divine. Precisely for that reason, it is inherently more dangerous than other forms of terrorism. As Prof. Boyer suggests, "extremism is simply an excessive form of religious adherence."[1]

The clearest manifestation of contemporary religious extremism is modern-day terrorism. While religion has been a prime motivator for acts of unconscionable violence committed against people of other religions throughout history, it has not been associated in the modern age—until recently—with terrorism. In past decades, terrorism has been more closely associated with ideological or national movements, yet today religion is the most widely cited motivation for terrorism.

With respect to extremist religious movements, the question is often asked—"Has religion been perverted when it is offered as justification for terrorist acts, or is religion itself inherently violent?" No matter how compelling, this question is somewhat irrelevant. The "purity" of the religion in question is not as important as how the individual in question views and manifests his or her religion.

The concept of religion is expansive; to claim that terrorists are motivated solely by religion does not offer much help in understanding either religion or terrorism. Terrorists can be motivated by different aspects of the same religion—a Muslim suicide bomber could be motivated by any of the following: the promise of paradise, the forgiveness for sins committed in this life, the restoration of family honor, or contribution to God's holy cause on earth. To say that religion is the motivation in all these different instances is true, but neither sufficiently nor satisfactorily specific.

It is critical to understand that the motivation to act in the name of God is not endemic only to Islam, for Christians and Jews have similarly committed terrorist acts on behalf of what they consider their God. Crusaders sought to "liberate" the Holy Land. Radical right-wing Christians bombed homosexual nightclubs and abortion clinics. Yigal Amir claimed he was carrying out the will of God when he assassinated Israeli Prime Minister Yitzhak Rabin. The Old Testament is bloody with countless victims of violent battles. The Qu'ran, while stressing that Islam is the religion of peace, exhorts its followers to be uncompromising in attacking those that deny Islam. While controversy rages as to whether *jihad*, or warfare on behalf of Islam, is defensive or offensive, the reality is that the Qu'ran is very clear with respect to a fundamental

---

1   Pascal Boyer, *Religion Explained: The Evolutionary Origins of Religious Thought* 292 (Basic Books, 2001).

message: kill the non-believer (external) and the hypocrite (internal).[2] Christians and Jews have similarly committed acts of terrorism predicated on "divine inspiration" and religious belief. The problem is not inherently religion; rather, it is the view of a religious extremist regarding his or her own belief system.

Extremists believe in the absolute supreme authority of their scripture—or, at least, what they understand to be their scripture. For religious extremists, compromise is unimaginable. Religion has priority over all other considerations—including morality and secular law—for the religious extremist. Even if those considerations include acts of violence. Whether the 72 vestal virgins promised to suicide bombers are actually described directly in the Qu'ran, or whether they are the product of urban legend is largely insignificant. Many aspiring suicide bombers believe this much-anticipated award awaits them. Extremists believe that scripture comes directly from God or God's prophets, and therefore words are to be taken literally. Since many scriptures contain passages that describe violence and revenge, these words offer both justifications and commandments to the extremist follower.

For the actor who believes in the infallibility of his or her religion, whether he or she possesses a profound understanding of religious scripture is not important. The key is that the individual's acts are performed "in the name of God." For example, in the case of Islam, the Qu'ran forbids both murder and suicide. What allows a suicide bomber to justify his or her actions on behalf of religion is framing the act in terms of "self-sacrifice" and martyrdom. Is this a correct interpretation of Islam? The majority view would say no. Yet arguing theology will not result in a safer society.

How terrorists view themselves, their enemies, their victims, and the nature of their conflict has a dramatic impact on motivation. To an extremist, members of their religion are among the chosen, the saved. Everyone else is destined for damnation. In a religion that describes everything as "us" and "them," what would otherwise be a purely political fight can literally be termed as conflict between good and evil.

Therefore, to the extremist religious terrorist, the victims of an attack are either innocent victims who will go straight to heaven, or collaborators with evil who deserve their fate. In either case, the actor need not worry

---

2   Rueven Firestone, *Jihad, The Origin of Holy War in Islam* 17 (Oxford University Press, 1999).

about the consequences or the implications. A religiously motivated terrorist feels perfectly justified in his or her actions. When confronted with threats and attacks predicated on religious extremism, governments must respond more forcefully and directly than in the past.

SECULAR LAW VERSUS RELIGIOUS LAW

Membership and participation in civil democratic society explicitly demands that citizens respect the rule of law as supreme. According to the logic of Rousseau, as citizens of a society we are all signatories to the grand social contract; in essence, we give up any truly *absolute* rights for the safety and comfort that government can provide. We agree to be subject to laws and regulations imposed by a civil society including regulations on religion, regardless of the fact that we typically consider religious rights to be absolute.

That is not to minimize the importance, relevance, or centrality of religion in the lives of untold millions. We simply must recognize that civil society is one whose essence is civil law rather than religious law. Some people of faith—particularly those for whom religion is the essence of their temporal existence—may find this perspective objectionable; however, civil society cannot endure if religious law is supreme to state law.

The proponents of such a theory must not only be the non-religious, but also members of minority religious groups. After all, what are Baptists, Jews, Muslims, and Buddhists to do in a society dominated by mainstream Protestants or Roman Catholics? Should they simply embrace the codification of Catholic law in civil life? Such a proposal would be met with extreme opposition, and rightly so. Even societies that embrace historical remnants of religious law and secular law have acknowledged this fact. For example, in the United Kingdom, where the monarch must be Anglican and swear to be the defender of the faith,[3] religious law cannot override civil law in the governance of citizens.

While religion may be important in forming mores and norms, it is not superior to state law—at least not in liberal Western democracies. Religion is not granted unlimited powers, or special rights. This statement holds true not only for religion as a conceptual institution, but also

---

3   SHIMON SHETREET, Religion in the Public Sphere: A Comparative Analysis of German, Israeli, American and International Law, *The Model of State and Church Relations and Its Impact on the Protection of Freedom of Conscience and Religion: A Comparative Study of Israel* 101 (2007).

for practitioners and theologians. An individual accused of violating a state's law should find little recourse in claiming that he or she was adhering to religious law. Despite this fundamental premise, there is little doubt that the concept of the supremacy of civil law is met with resistance in numerous quarters worldwide.

A discussion about civil law prompts questions regarding its origin. Civil laws are imposed on citizens to protect society; change in these laws is inevitable. Such change reflects modernity and improvement of society; expanding civil liberties to previously disenfranchised individuals is a prime example. *How* the change occurs is critical. Is the change predicated on violence and the unwarranted deprivation of civil and political rights? If so, the change is most likely a negative force in society. Conversely, if change is effectuated through the democratic process, then it more likely reflects the will of the people and advances society.[4] This is in direct contrast to religious law, thought to be governed by God and therefore unalterable by man. Civil democratic regimes are endangered when religious extremists—violently or through dangerous intimidation—seek to impose religious law on civil society precisely because religious law is not subject to democratic referendum.

History is replete with example acts of violence committed in the name of God against non-believers, heretics, or innocent bystanders when people of faith have sought to impose religious will on secular society. Violence on behalf of a deity is fundamentally different from secular or nationalist violence. Religious extremism, when combined with nationalist fervor, has the greatest potential to undermine the essence of democratic societies. Unlike democratic values, which are fundamentally encompassing,[5] religious extremists seek to impose a narrow, dogmatic interpretation of their religious scripture on civil society. There is an enormous danger to civil society predicated on the absoluteness with which religious extremists seek to impose their beliefs. Furthermore, religious extremism is often initially practiced privately, thereby sheltering it from the censure of society at large. As a result, the public may be

---

4   This is not to suggest that popular will might not at times result in unjust laws that damage society—however, as a general statement, popular opinion over time will result in positive change for society.

5   Though, obviously, history is replete with democracies consistently and systematically seeking to deprive the rights of minority populations; the American Deep South is a vivid example of systematic institutionalized violations of political and civil rights.

caught unaware when religious extremism results in actual violence. While democracies must allow for tolerance of religion within society, they cannot allow religious extremists to endanger society itself. Therefore, governments must be wary of religious conduct and speech, constantly examining its potential to endanger civil society.

EXTREMIST RELIGION AND ABSOLUTIST REGIMES

In discussing the question of religious-based violence, the inevitable comparison to non-religious violence is raised. Is the belief in supremacy of faith different than the belief in supremacy of mass movements? Is death in the name of a God different than death in the name of ideology? Is religion simply another form of "absolutism," indistinguishable from mass movements that have wreaked well-documented havoc throughout history?

The Rev. Dr. John Lentz observed:

> In general religion is not, by definition, another form of absolutism. However, any religious perspective that seeks to control behavior of believers, limits the access to other points of view, and demands strict adherence to a particular world-view, code of ethics, or manner of living moves along the trajectory toward absolute control and is hardly distinguishable from other forms of political or social absolutism.[6]

It is not the intention of this book to engage in "religion bashing." This point cannot be sufficiently emphasized, as the bashing of religion—as others have done—is both offensive to people of faith and does not make a contribution to the discussion that we must have regarding the danger posed by religious extremism. Rather, it detracts from the debate for it engages in demagoguery and populism.

It is important to emphasize that millions of people have been killed for purely non-religious reasons. Prime examples include Nazism, Italian Fascism, Pol Pot, and the Cultural Revolution. All four regimes (Germany, Italy, Cambodia, and China) were marked by absolute loyalty to the state and its leaders. In fulfilling real or perceived loyalty requirements, citizens of those regimes committed mass murder on an unparalleled scale.

The concept of religious superiority has led individuals of faith throughout history to commit horrific acts of violence against two categories of

---

6   Email communication between the Rev. Dr. John C. Lentz Jr. and the author, June 17, 2008.

non-believers—those who are nominally members of the same faith, but whose fervency is doubted by the actor, and those of other faiths. Does that differ from individuals who believe in the supremacy of a secular belief, such as communism? Is there something specific about religious supremacy that significantly distinguishes it from secular movement supremacy?

In many ways, the two are similar, yet religious extremists differ in several important respects. The doctrine of certitude[7] proposes that religious actors are (1) certain of a deity, and (2) certain that they are acting in the name of that deity. Certitude, then, is a two-step process that requires the believer to fully internalize both belief in a higher power, and the requirement of action on behalf of a higher power. Otherwise the religious belief is not absolute. Furthermore, religious belief is predicated on the notion that *its* deity is supreme. The certainty of religious extremists is also played out in the relationship between authority figures and their followers. A religious extremist authority figure can be perceived as the voice of God on earth, able to compel followers in ways that the leader of an extremist political organization may not.

But does that necessarily make religious extremists more dangerous to society than secular extremists? In the last century, secular extremists have been arguably more numerous, and their actions have had far greater impact on the modern nation-state. The more appropriate question is, given the choice between absolute devotion to a secular cause and absolute certainty in extremist religious beliefs, which of the two presents the greatest danger to society today? The appropriate conclusion based on an analysis of contemporary terrorism is that religious extremists pose a greater threat to society than secular extremists. While that does not mean that religion is always the answer to the question of what is the greatest danger facing society, it is undeniable that religious extremists pose a danger that must be responded to legislatively, politically, and if need be, forcefully.

HOW CAN RELIGIOUS RIGHTS BE LIMITED?

To protect civil democratic society, religious rights need to be curtailed. In the American paradigm, constitutionally guaranteed rights are not absolute. Each right may be subject to narrowly tailored limitations when a compelling state interest is implicated. If religious rights *may*, under

---

7   Phrase used in private conversation with author, details in author's records.

some circumstances, be limited, the question is whether the government *must*, under other circumstances, limit those religious rights to protect members of society.

The dilemma that must be addressed is what the limits of otherwise-guaranteed rights are.

The easy response is that rights must be limited when they "run afoul of the law." Yet, this is an unsatisfactory answer, not only because of the numerous examples of extremist religious violence, but also because governments are often hesitant to enforce laws against religious actors. Governments should be willing to curtail certain acts of religious extremism if they are deemed to potentially endanger other members of society, whether that endangerment takes places on a national level, local level, or is directed toward a member of the "internal community."[8]

When discussing the limitation of rights, it is critical to define terms. *Religious belief* is a personal experience; *Religious practice* is how religious belief manifests itself;[9] *prayer* is the manner in which a person of faith communicates with his or her deity; *speech* is communication by a person of faith or religious leader (priest, imam, rabbi) to other persons of faith and/or non-religious individuals, invoking the deity for the purpose of action in the name of religion.

Private religion is the manifestation of the above in any combination within the home. Belief, practice, and speech with respect to religion within the confines of the home represents an effective balance between the state and individual rights; individuals have the right to believe, practice, and speak about religion within the confines of their home without limitation (unless such practice involves illegal conduct). Private religion protects non-believers from religion; non-believers need not enter a private home and thus not be subjected to the religion. *Public religion*, however, not only affects the delicate balance between the state and the individual, it also conceivably endangers the now vulnerable non-believer. The state, in response, will be forced to protect the non-believer. One of the manners in which the state will protect the non-believer is by limiting the freedoms of the believer.

---

8   The reference is to internal communities such as The Fundamentalist Church of Jesus Christ of Latter-Day Saints (FLDS). For background discussion on the FLDS, see the Appendix.

9   *See* Michael W. McConnell, *The Origins and Historical Understanding of Free Exercise of Religion*, 103 HARV. L. REV. 1409 (1990).

The extent to which these rights should be limited is a legitimate and necessary conversation. The right to believe in a particular religion is protected by international law, national constitutions, and domestic law (for example, Basic Laws in the Israeli model, the Religious Freedom Restoration Act in the United States). When discussing rights with respect to religion, we must specifically refer to rights associated with the practice of religious *extremism*—when the actor believes that his or her tenets and principles are infallible and that *any* action, even violence, taken on behalf of those beliefs is justified.

In addition, serious consideration should be given as to whether conduct commonly associated with religious extremism should be similarly curtailed. An interesting test case is the headscarves worn by Muslim women. The reactions of governments have run the gamut from ignoring the headscarf (United States and particularly the United Kingdom) to a partial ban (Turkey). This inconsistency in how to respond to a piece of cloth demonstrates the inherent difficulty of confronting this issue. The headscarf *potentially* represents something profoundly dangerous to some, while to others it is but a public manifestation of modesty and devotion. The issue of the headscarf will be discussed further[10] and ultimately it will be shown that states that have sought to restrict such religious expression are guilty not only of governmental excess at the expense of personal liberty, but may have inadvertently contributed to even greater religious extremism.

In examining these potential threats it must be acknowledged that there is the inherent danger of excess when government responds to public pressure. The internment of Japanese-Americans in the aftermath of the attack on Pearl Harbor and the Supreme Court's subsequent ruling in *Korematsu*[11] are prime examples of governmental overreaction. The Military Commissions established by President Bush in the aftermath of 9/11, where individuals can be detained without any guaranteed rights, is a more recent example of executive excess in the face of a threat.

As an additional example, a leading Israeli academic[12] suggests examining the reaction of Israeli authorities to demonstrations opposed to the

---

10   *See* Chapter 7; for background and further discussion of the headscarf in Turkey, see the Appendix.

11   *Korematsu v. United States*, 324 U.S. 885 (1945).

12   Private conversation with the author, June 12, 2008; details in the author's records.

government's decision to disengage from the Gaza Strip.[13] During the course of the demonstrations, 250 citizens were arrested. Seventy were released shortly after arrest, while 180 were detained for refusing to give their names and addresses.[14] These arrests represent classic overreaction both to free assembly and to free speech. This overreaction can be just as dangerous to society as the threat that extremist religion poses; therefore the decision to limit guaranteed rights must be made extremely carefully.

THREATS FROM EXTREMIST RELIGION

The practice of religion involves three separate, yet intertwined elements: *belief*, *speech*, and *conduct*. In considering imposing limits on these elements, policy-makers and the public alike must define what threat, if any, religious extremism presents to national security and public order. The threat analysis requires defining the tolerable level of threat acceptable to the state and its citizens. If viewed on a spectrum or sliding scale, *belief* is the most private and intimate of the three aspects of religiosity, and therefore the least subject to the imposition of limitations. Conversely, *speech* and *conduct* are the most visible manifestations of religion.

Belief does not present a threat to the state; belief is internal and protected. *Speech*, however, raises different concerns. A member of the clergy speaking negatively about another faith does not inherently endanger national security. That speech does not necessarily endanger believers in the "other" religion. However, if that same faith leader were to combine his critical comments with a call to action, be it explicit or implicit from the listener's perspective, then there may be a viable threat to national security.

In determining whether the faith leader's speech is to be viewed as a viable threat, it is incumbent to determine the capability of listeners to carry out the message. That is, while words can clearly be dangerous, it is also important to assess whether a congregant in the faith leader's

---

13   August 2005, resulting in the dismantling of Jewish settlements in the Gaza Strip directly affecting the 10,000 Jews who lived there and were subsequently forced to live elsewhere (either in Israel or the West Bank). The decision to dismantle was initiated by then Prime Minister Sharon and approved by the government in a vote. Petitions were filed to the Supreme Court sitting as the High Court of Justice; all were denied.

14   The Guardian, July 22, 2005; 250 were arrested as three-day Gaza settler protest ends, Conal Urquhart.

community can actually act on those words. The question that must be asked is whether the words represent an "operational" threat. As it is difficult to assess the "operational capability" of each and every worshipper, criteria for assessing whether extremist religious speech is incitement must be broadened. The criteria must include analysis both of the relationship between the faith leader and his community and whether his words have been previously acted upon. This recommended test will apply regardless of the congregation's size and will be viable only if law enforcement officials are convinced that worshippers are prone to violence based on the faith leader's words.[15]

Conduct, in furtherance of a belief may present a threat, and therefore is limitable. In 1878, the Supreme Court held that federal law prohibiting polygamy did not violate the Free Exercise rights of a Mormon who claimed polygamy a fundamental tenet of his faith.[16] Belief remained untouched—but acting on that belief was appropriately curtailed. Similarly in *Employment Div., Dept. of Human Resources of State of Oregon v. Smith*, the Supreme Court ruled that even if peyote were used as part of a religious ceremony, it was proper for Oregon to deny unemployment benefits to those fired for using the drug.[17] Following the *Reynolds* and *Smith* rulings to their logical conclusion, in the context of religious extremism, religious beliefs should be protected, but religiously inspired conduct need not necessarily be protected.

LEGAL PROTECTION FOR RELIGIOUS FREEDOMS

The United Kingdom, the Netherlands, and Turkey are all signatories to the European Convention on Human Rights (ECHR), which guarantees the right to religious freedom.[18] Similarly, the national constitutions, case law, and relevant legislation[19] of the five surveyed nations guarantee that same right. The ECHR was drafted in an effort to secure

---

15   Private correspondence between a reader of an earlier draft and the author, comments in author's records.

16   *Reynolds v. United States*, 98 U.S. 145 (1878).

17   *Employment Div., Dept. of Human Resources of State of Oregon v. Smith*, 485 U.S. 660 (1988).

18   European Convention on Human Rights, Art. 9(1).

19   Of the five surveyed nations, the U.S., the Netherlands, and Turkey have constitutions; Israel has Basic Laws and the UK has sources such as the parliamentary constitutional conventions.

the universal and effective recognition and observances of rights, and expresses a desire to ensure that individuals have the right to practice (extending beyond mere belief) their religion. That right, however, while essential to the human existence cannot, and must not, lead to the killing either of non-believers or individuals accused of turning against their own religion.

There are two commands to which a person of faith must adhere—the demands of his or her state, and the demands of his or her religion. As Prof. Paul Cliteur has compellingly suggested, "moderate believers tell us they 'do not see' any contradiction between living in the modern world and their religion. . . . the growth of religious extremists contradicts their sanguine attitude."[20] How to resolve this tension is not new;[21] however, contemporary religious extremism requires this question be re-engaged. Doing so requires stating that otherwise-guaranteed rights will not be fully respected in the context of protecting society from religious extremism. Perhaps it is appropriate in discussing this issue to ask whether states can afford the ideal. As Justice Jackson wrote in his dissent in *Terminiello v. Chicago*,[22] the "Constitution is not a suicide pact." By analogy, the same cautionary approach can be applied to international conventions that strive to protect both religion and people of faith.

But even if we reach the conclusion that fundamental rights may be limited in order to protect civil society, we are left with the question— *How*? What is the correct response when religious extremists present immediate threats to civil democratic society? Government's fundamental obligation is to protect the public from external and internal threats alike. While non-democratic regimes have traditionally viewed religion as a threat—after all, anti-religion doctrine was a core principal of Communist ideology[23]—democratic states have historically articulated principles of religious freedom.

Yet it is imperative to emphasize that the religious tolerance attributed to European nations was limited to Christianity—and even this tolerance

---

20 E-mail in author's records.

21 *See* Micah 6:8, "What does the Lord require of you? But to do justice, love kindness and walk humbly before your God."

22 *Terminiello v. Chicago*, 337 U.S. 1 (1949).

23 *See* David Kowalewski, *Protest for Religious Rights in the USSR: Characteristics and Consequences*, 39 RUSSIAN REVIEW 4 (1980).

was historically limited at times, leaving either Protestants or Catholics outside society's protection. In addition, Islam had not been a part of the western European landscape from the early 1600s until the 20th century,[24] while anti-Semitism has been a blight on Europe for centuries. In addressing religious freedom in Europe, it is important to note that freedom was extended exclusively to the majority religion with limited, if any, protection extended to minority religions.

AN AMERICAN EXAMPLE: THE FUNDAMENTALIST CHURCH OF JESUS CHRIST OF LATTER-DAY SAINTS

The FLDS church has its roots in one of America's great religious movements—Mormonism, or The Church of Jesus Christ of Latter-Day Saints (LDS). The FLDS church was formed in the early 1900s when individuals broke away from the LDS church after it renounced the practice of polygamy and excommunicated practitioners of plural marriage. Since breaking away, the FLDS Church has become increasingly radicalized in its beliefs and practices. While FLDS will be discussed in greater detail in Chapter Seven, it is mentioned here to illustrate that religious extremism exists in America. Furthermore, as illustrated by the FLDS, religious extremists do not only pose a threat to society at-large, but to members of their own community as well. Whether it is Muslim extremists who kill their daughters, sisters, and wives for dishonoring their families, or FLDS families who marry off their underage daughters to middle aged men, governments must be aware of the danger that extremists pose to the most vulnerable members of society—the unprotected victims.

THE NETHERLANDS: AHMED MARCOUCH

The Netherlands has experienced violence based on religious extremism in recent years. The murder of Theo van Gogh, a Dutch columnist, filmmaker, and social critic, brutally stabbed to death in Amsterdam by Mohammed Bouyeri after making an anti-Islam film with Ayaan Hirsi Ali, *Submission*, is but the most obvious and violent example. In 2008, Ahmed Marcouch, District Mayor of Slotervaart, Amsterdam, went on national television and stated that Islam "must come to terms with homosexuality."[25] Marcouch further said that full assimilation into

---

24   *See* Albert Hourani, *History of the Arab Peoples* (Faber & Faber, 2002).

25   *Pauw & Witteman Show* (VARA Broadcasting, April 2, 2008).

Dutch political society would only be possible for Islamic immigrants who sought gainful employment and learned Dutch.[26] Shortly thereafter, Marcouch announced that Sheikh Fawaz Jneid, a radical imam of the As-Soenna mosque in The Hague, had issued a *fatwa*[27] against him, and that his life was in danger. While Jneid denied issuing a fatwa, *The Volkskrant*, a Dutch daily newspaper, published an open letter from Marcouch to Jneid, challenging him to rescind the *fatwa* and openly debate the issues.

So how should the Dutch government have responded to Jneid's alleged *fatwa*? Marcouch himself has proposed a legislative ban on *fatwas*. A *fatwa* is an opinion on Islamic law, issued by an Islamic scholar. Its strength ranges from non-binding to persuasive to fully authoritative, depending on the scholar and the audience. Initially, it would seem that a ban on all *fatwas* would be too broad a response. After all, a *fatwa* could reinforce the equality of the sexes, encourage devout Muslims to adopt children, or exhort followers to exhibit more charity in their personal lives.

Yet it is clear that *fatwas* are also used by extremist Muslims to promote violence. Would it be a more fair legislative response to only ban *fatwas* with "objectionable" messages—a content-based restriction on freedom of speech? While such a response might be more "fair," it could be legally problematic. The question that will be repeatedly asked throughout this book is whether the extreme actions of a few should affect how millions of non-extremist believers are able to practice their faith. Is religion that much of a threat? Or is this very premise an exaggeration, prompting a nervous response to the actions of a misguided few? Ultimately, this book's thesis is that religion is indistinguishable from any other threat facing the state. Religion does not have immunity either from criticism or from proactive limitation.

---

26   Nederlandse Moslim Omroep (Dutch Muslim Group) broadcast on April 13, 2008, *available at* http://player.omroep.nl/?aflid=6862069&start=00:09:57&end=00:18:03, last viewed July 10, 2008.

27   A *fatwa* is a religious opinion on Islamic law; perhaps the most famous *fatwa* was issued by the Ayatollah Khamenei against the writer Salman Rushdie for his book *The Satanic Verses* which Khamenei believed offensive to the Islamic faith. The *fatwa* imposed a death sentence on Rushdie; http://news.bbc.co.uk/onthisday/hi/dates/stories/december/26/newsid_2542000/2542873.stm, last viewed June 6, 2009.

THE TURKISH EXPERIENCE

Whether Turkey becomes what some commentators have termed "Islamized" is that country's most pressing current policy issue. The question is obviously relevant to Turks but also has significant geo-political implications, given Turkey's pivotal geographical location (straddling two continents) and its significant natural resources. Numerous discussions with security analysts in different countries make Turkey's geo-political importance very clear. As one senior Western official stated, "the West cannot afford to lose Turkey."[28] He went on: "An Islamized Turkey endangers both European and Middle East stability—endangers because of its size, location and military superiority."[29]

Central to the recent secular-religious debate in Turkey are symbolic issues, such as the recent controversy over headscarves. In February 2008, Turkey lifted its ban on wearing headscarves in schools; the ban had been in place since 1980.[30] However, on June 5, 2008, the Turkish Constitutional Court canceled the constitutional amendments that lifted the ban, ruling that "the Turkish Parliament had violated the constitutionally enshrined principle of secularism when it passed amendments to lift the headscarf ban on university campuses."[31] Islamists who supported lifting the ban viewed the Parliament's decision as a move toward religious freedom, claiming that the lift would "end the sufferings of our girls at university gates . . . in reference to pious female students who have been forced to remove their head scarves at the entrance to campuses."[32] However, since the lift was overturned, those supporters question whether "[t]his decision means that women who choose to wear a headscarf in Turkey will be forced to choose between their religion

---

28   Private conversation with author, June, 2008; identity known to author.

29   *Id.*

30   Sabrina Tavernise, *Turkey's Parliament Votes to Lift Head Scarf Ban*, NEW YORK TIMES, February 9, 2008, *available at* http://www.nytimes.com/2008/02/09/world/europe/09cnd-turkey.html, last visited December 1, 2008.

31   Kandy Ringer, *Religion and Expression Rights Denied, Broader Reform Agenda Endangered*, BBC NEWS, June 9, 2008, *available at* http://bbsnews.net/article.php/2008060920331197, last visited December 1, 2008.

32   *Turkish Law Makers vote to Lift Headscarf Ban*, MSNBC World News, February 9, 2008, *available at* http://www.msnbc.msn.com/id/23081329/, last visited July 5, 2008.

and their education."[33] Others who supported the ban, such as members of the Republican People's party, viewed the headscarf as a political symbol of the "dark ages,"[34] and as a move toward "the death of the secular republic."[35]

The secular vs. religious debate has become a central issue in Turkey's current political scene. The president of Turkey is thought to be the guardian of secularism passed down from Mustafa Kemal Atatürk, Turkey's first President.[36] However, the most recent election was marked by protest and controversy, as many called the protection of secularism into question with the election of the Justice and Development Party, (APK) the Islamic-oriented party. In March 2008, "a closure case was filed against the ruling party . . . on claims that it became the focal point of anti-secular activities."[37] In a controversial ruling, the Constitutional Court declined to close down the party. According to a Turkey-focused U.S. news service, "Hasim Kilic, the court chairman, said the court was still sending the party a 'serious warning' by cutting half of the treasury funds it was entitled to this year."[38]

Discussing the question of religion in the Turkish context requires analyzing secular Islam as compared to religious Islam. The overwhelming majority of Turks, approximately 99.8 percent, are Muslim, mostly Sunni, while the remaining 0.2 percent are either Christians or Jews.[39] However,

---

33   Holly Cartner, Europe and Central Asia director at Human Rights Watch, Kandy Ringer, *Religion and Expression Rights Denied, Broader Reform Agenda Endangered*, BBC NEWS, June 9, 2008, *available at* http://bbsnews.net/article.php/2008060920331197, last visited December 1, 2008.

34   *Turkish Law Makers vote to Lift Headscarf Ban*, MSNBC World News, February 9, 2008, *available at* http://www.msnbc.msn.com/id/23081329/, last visited July 5, 2008.

35   *Turkish Law Makers vote to Lift Headscarf Ban*, MSNBC World News, February 9, 2008, *available at* http://www.msnbc.msn.com/id/23081329/, last visited July 5, 2008.

36   For further information on the history of secularism in Turkey, see the Appendix.

37   *Turkey's Top Court Rules Not to Close the Ruling Party*, TURKS.US, July 30, 2008, *available at* http://www.turks.us/article.php?story=20080730113627683, last visited December 1, 2008.

38   *Id.*

39   CIA World Fact Book, Turkey, *available at* https://www.cia.gov/library/publications/the-world-factbook/geos/tu.html#People, last visited July 7, 2008.

not all Muslims are *religious* Muslims, and not all believe that Turkey should or must be an Islamic state. However, discussions with Turkish and non-Turkish experts alike[40] lead one to conclude that even if Turkey does not adopt Shar'ia law, religiosity will play an increasingly influential role in determining Turkish domestic and international policy.

What does increasing religiousness in Turkey suggest? As one Turkish commentator suggested to me, "If Turkey becomes religious, secular Muslims will not be promoted to positions of national importance and will not play a role in defining Turkey."[41] The political marginalization of secular Turks may result in discrimination, if not outright violence, against those opposed to a theocratic Turkey. On a geo-political level, Turkey's foreign affairs will be impacted and perhaps even dominated by the religious beliefs, conduct, and principles of Islam.

CONCLUSION: HOW CAN SOCIETY LIMIT RELIGION?

Freedom of conscience is one of the most fundamental aspects of a democratic society. Such freedom includes the right to speak about religion, to assemble on behalf of religion, to practice religion, to associate with fellow believers and exclude nonbelievers. The following chapters will address each of these issues, and provide recommendations as to how liberal governments should respond to the threat of religious extremism while protecting guaranteed rights.

The danger, however, in responding to threats of extremism is in violating constitutional rights. Why, after all, should teenage girls in Paris be banned from wearing a headscarf? Does the scarf—in and of itself—threaten society? Are secular Muslims, much less Jews and Christians, threatened by the scarf? Why in London are Muslims not banned from wearing the scarf? Why in the Netherlands is there an increasing concern regarding Islam? Does increasing religiosity in Turkey both threaten Turkish domestic society and impact larger geo-political considerations? Does the possibility that the religious right in Israel return to its unparalleled and unrestrained incitement prior to Rabin's assassination endanger Israeli society? Does the conduct of FLDS threaten *only* the teenage brides (internal community) or is the broader (external) community undermined because of widespread internal polygamy combined with forced sexual relations involving female minors? Does the FLDS Church

---

40   Private conversations with author; identities known to author.

41   Private conversations with author; identities known to author.

present a danger different to American society than right-wing pastors encouraging their congregants to kill abortion-performing physicians?

While the above societies are not in danger that their immediate stability is at risk, I do suggest that the power of religious extremism raises significant questions concerning the limits of rights. To *not* address them is to gainsay reality. The question we must address is the confluence of religious extremism and national security; stated differently, does religious extremism affect the national security of the five surveyed nations? The reflexive answer is no; the more thoughtful response suggests there are sufficient indications that the question merits serious discussion.

With all the appropriate disclaimers behind us, the following chapters address in detail the issues raised in this chapter. Easy answers to complicated questions are not the order of the day for any discussion addressing possible limitations of otherwise granted rights. Such a discussion raises significant judicial and ethical concerns. Society is at risk from religious extremism, demanding serious discussion regarding what measures are to be taken to minimize the threat. If civil societies are to effectively combat the threat posed by religious extremists, these questions must be answered.

CHAPTER THREE

THE LIMITS OF FREEDOM OF SPEECH

INTRODUCTION: DEFINING RELIGIOUS SPEECH

A critical component of democracy is the value placed on civil and political rights. Foremost among these rights is the freedom of speech. Governments recognize the right to free speech—for example, the U.S. Constitution enshrines the right to free speech in the First Amendment— and multi-national agreements such as the International Covenant on Civil and Political Rights (ICCPR) recognize it as well. The right to practice religion freely is similarly valued by democracies. These rights are something just short of sacrosanct; all democracies recognize that certain limits may be placed on these rights. For example, U.S. law recognizes a difference between protected speech and unprotected speech (libel, obscenity, incitement, fighting words).

The question is whether religious speech deserves additional protection because it encompasses two separate individual rights. This is an easy intellectual assumption to make. After all, the freedom of religion and the freedom of speech are two of the most important rights enjoyed by members of democratic societies. Many might assume that, given the importance of these two rights, that they become exponentially more important when in combination. Given that speech is already highly protected, does this mean that religious-based speech is to receive near total immunity?

Yet does not treating religious speech as "extra protected" create a problem as secular individuals will never enjoy this heightened protection? Prof. Fred Gedicks noted, "It is difficult to argue today that religious interests are inherently more worthy of protection than morally comparable secular interests."[1] This view is articulated in the Netherlands where religious speech enjoys the same rights as secular speech, but not more. Similarly, the Turkish constitution specifically allows for freedom of

---

1   *See* Frederick Mark Gedicks, *Three Questions about Hybrid Rights and Religious Groups*, 117 YALE L.J. Pocket Part 192 (2008), http://thepocketpart.org/2008/03/24/gedicks.html.

speech, but defines the limits that must be followed.[2] So perhaps religious speech is simply the *exact same* as all other speech, and should be subject to the same legal analysis—and limitation—as any other statement or written document.

This seemingly innocent premise must be thoroughly examined. As discussed in the previous chapter, the danger posed by religious extremists to civil society is significant. The religious extremist believes in the infallibility of his or her belief system, and such a worldview leads the actor to believe in absolutes, to reject compromise, and to express indifference to alternative opinions. Furthermore, the relationship between figures of authority and followers is acutely different in the religious context. A religious authority figure is viewed as a representative of God on earth. A follower is far more likely to act on the words of a religious authority figure than other speakers. Does this not suggest that in some cases, society and government should view religious speech as inherently *less protected* than secular political speech because of its extraordinary ability to influence the listener?

This suggestion, problematic and potentially offensive, must be addressed in a world where religious extremism poses the gravest threat to national security and individuals.

According to the ICCPR, all member countries are required to prohibit any advocacy of national, racial, or religious hatred that constitutes incitement to discrimination, hostility, or violence.[3] The U.S. has long been hesitant to curb any free speech, fearing a violation of the First Amendment. However, even the greatest advocates of the freedom of speech have drawn "a line in the sand" that should not be crossed. Great American legal minds including Judge Learned Hand,[4] Justice Oliver

---

2   Penal Code, Republic of Turkey, Article 301 (2005).

3   ICCPR, Article 20.

4   *Masses Pub. Co. v. Patten*, 244 F. 535, 540 (S.D.N.Y. 1917). "Political agitation, by the passions it arouses or the convictions it engenders, may in fact stimulate men to the violation of the law. Detestation of existing policies is easily transformed into forcible resistance of the authority which puts them in execution, and it would be folly to disregard the causal relation between the two. Yet to assimilate agitation, legitimate as such, with direct incitement to violent resistance, is to disregard the tolerance of all methods of political agitation which in normal times is a safeguard of free government."–Judge Learned Hand

Wendell Holmes,[5] and Justice Louis Brandeis[6] have conceded that the government could limit any speaker who would counsel an individual or a group to commit an unlawful act.[7] Only the most absolute advocates of free speech, such as Hugo Black, advocated never limiting free speech.[8]

What is *religious speech*? Is religious speech any speech that references religion? Or must the speech meet some degree of theological relevance before it becomes religious speech? To complicate the matter even further, is speech only communication (verbal or written) or can certain speech be expansively viewed as conduct? While some may argue that the distinction is artificial, this book defines *religious speech* as that which is verbally spoken or written, and defines conduct as that which falls under the category of "exercise" of religion.[9]

In arguing that some religious speech must be considered *less* protected than other speech, what exactly does that mean? Faith-based, religious speech does not automatically warrant infringement on free speech. It is when that speech becomes something else—something that threatens other individuals—that we must begin to consider the possibility that religious speech can no longer hide behind the shield of freedom of expression. Engaging in this discussion requires defining and analyzing

---

5   *Schenck v. Unites States*, 249 U.S. 39, 52 (1919). "The question in every case is whether the words used are used in such circumstances and are of such a nature as to create a clear and present danger that they will bring about the substantive evils that Congress has a right to prevent."–Justice Holmes

6   *Whitney v. California*, 274 U.S. 357 (1927). "To justify suppression of free speech, there must be reasonable ground to fear that serious evil will result if free speech is practiced. There must be reasonable ground to believe that the danger apprehended is imminent."–Justice Brandeis

7   *Masses Pub. Co. v. Patten*, 244 F. 535, 540 (S.D.N.Y. 1917).

8   *Dennis et al. v. U.S.* 341 U.S. 494 (1951) "So long as this Court exercises the power of judicial review of legislation, I cannot agree that the First Amendment permits us to sustain laws suppressing freedom of speech and press on the basis of Congress's or our own notions of mere 'reasonableness'. Such a doctrine waters down the First Amendment so that it amounts to little more than an admonition to Congress. The Amendment as so construed is not likely to protect any but those 'safe' or orthodox views which rarely need its protection. . . ." However, it must also be noted Black did support limiting the obscene, which he termed "non-speech".

9   This issue will be further discussed in Chapter Seven in the context of the headscarf worn by Muslim women.

what is a threat and when is it actionable. That is, when does a threat become criminal incitement? To address this question, we will turn to an examination of a relatively recent example of religious speech becoming criminal incitement: the assassination of Yitzak Rabin.

ISRAEL: THE ASSASSINATION OF YITZAK RABIN

In 1992, Yitzhak Rabin was elected Prime Minister of Israel. Shortly thereafter, public and secret peace talks were initiated with the Palestine Liberation Organization (PLO). In September of 1993, Rabin, Yaser Arafat and U.S. President Bill Clinton signed the Oslo Accords on the White House lawn. Negotiated implementation[10] between Israeli and Palestinian representatives, under American auspices, began shortly thereafter.[11]

Rabin had concluded that the Israeli occupation of the West Bank and Gaza Strip[12] had caused Israeli society enormous damage morally, financially, and strategically. Rabin's decision to end the occupation was predicated on his belief that "benign occupation"[13] was a fiction. The relationship between Rabin—who served as Defense Minister in successive Israeli governments—and the settler[14] movement was problematic at best. On at least one occasion, Rabin called the settlers a "cancer" on Israeli society.[15]

---

10   The first stage was entitled "Gaza-Jericho Agreement", intended to facilitate transfer of power to the newly established Palestinian Authority both in the Gaza Strip and the city of Jericho.

11   The author was involved in "on the ground" implementation of the Accords in the Gaza Strip (1994–1999).

12   As a result of the 1967 Six-Day War, Israel came to occupy the West Bank and the Gaza Strip.

13   The term is credited to former Minister of Defense, Moshe Dayan.

14   The term "settler" refers to Jews who live in the West Bank.

15   Rabin believed one of his greatest mistakes as Prime Minister was failing to order the closing of the small but hostile and provocative Jewish settlement in Hebron after the 1994 attack on Palestinian worshippers in the Tomb of the Patriarchs. In that attack, Dr. Baruch Goldstein killed 29 Palestinians and wounded another 100 before the surviving worshippers killed him. Goldstein, a religious Jew, was a member of the extreme right-wing Kahanist movement.

Therefore Rabin decided to negotiate withdrawal both of the IDF[16] and Jewish settlers[17] from the West Bank and the Gaza Strip. The Accords were met with strident, consistent and angry opposition by the political and religious right in Israel, who believed that further compromise by Rabin endangered Jewish settlements in the West Bank. During 1995, inflammatory demonstrations were held in Israel when protestors displayed mock photographs of Rabin in Nazi S.S. uniforms. Politicians[18] from the political right joined forces with the religious right. Politicized, Orthodox rabbis virulently denounced Rabin. Incitement against Rabin became a daily reality in Israel. On November 4, 1995, Yigal Amir, a right-wing Israeli radical opposed to the Oslo Accords, assassinated Rabin. A minority of extremists termed the killing "heavenly retribution."[19]

Hate was in the air prior to the assassination; the violent sentiment was palpable and the primary agitators were rabbis. This sort of charged, frenzied atmosphere occurred in a modern democracy among seemingly rational individuals—and could occur again[20]—necessitating a careful

---

16 A military government had been established in the West Bank and Gaza Strip in the immediate aftermath of the Six-Day War under the command of a military governor; Israel never annexed the West Bank and Gaza Strip.

17 Successive Israeli governments (Likud and Labor alike) have encouraged, fostered and provided literally endless resources in the building of Jewish settlements in the West Bank and Gaza Strip. There are, today, at least 100,000 Jews living in the West Bank. Pre-disengagement from the Gaza Strip (in 2005), 10,000 Jews lived there.

18 Amongst the politicians who were most vehement in their opposition to the Accords and most extreme in their criticism of Rabin were then MP Netanyahu (subsequently elected Prime Minister), Sharon (subsequently elected Prime Minister), and Katsav (subsequently elected President).

19 Elliot Jager, *Thirteen Years After the Assassination, Wounds Still Fester*, The Jewish Exponent, November 20, 2008, *available at* http://www.jewishexponent.com/article/17647/.

20 As noted in the Introduction, I interviewed and met with scores of individuals in the course of researching and writing this book. With respect to these two questions—can the Israeli religious right incite to kill another Israeli Prime Minister and can a "true believer" carry out the words of his/her rabbi—many (but clearly not all) I interviewed in Israel responded in the negative. Nevertheless, in applying the triangle this book proposes (religious extremism/national security/legal analysis), the more realistic—I suggest—answer is somewhere between "perhaps" and "yes". That analysis "drives" this section.

examination of the nature of religious speech. For two years prior to the assassination, extreme right-wing rabbis issued a variety of proclamations regarding Rabin. Rabbi Shmuel Dvir, a teacher in the Har Etzion Yeshiva, told his students that it was "definitely permissible to kill Rabin under the provision of *din rodef*."[21] *Din rodef* is the duty of a Jew to kill a Jew who imperils the life or property of another Jew.[22] Dvir even boasted to one of his students, "If Rabin comes to visit Gush Etzion, I myself will climb on a roof and shoot him with a rifle."[23]

The International Rabbinical Coalition for Israel, an organization of Orthodox rabbis, declared Rabin a *rodef*, a Jew who deserved to be killed because he imperiled the life or property of another Jew.[24] The ultra-orthodox weekly paper, *Hashavna*, published a symposium issue addressing not only whether Rabin should be executed, but the most appropriate method to carry out the killing.[25] These are but a few of the examples of the extremist religious speech that directly encouraged violence against Rabin.

In the run-up to Rabin's assassination, *pulsa denura* was issued against him—a call to kill the Prime Minister because of his decision to pursue the Oslo peace process. The *pulsa denura*, translated as "lashes of fire," has long been a tradition of Kabbalah, a sect within Judaism. On the eve of Yom Kippur 1995, rabbis gathered on the sidewalk in front of Rabin's home after midnight to recite the ancient execration of *pulsa denura*. These 10 rabbis were disciples of the late Rabbi Meir Kahane. Avigdor Eskin, the group's leader, intoned, "I deliver to you, angel of wrath and ire, Yitzhak, the son of Rosa Rabin, that you may smother him and the specter of him, and cast him into bed, and dry up his wealth, and plague

21   Allan C. Brownfeld, *Israel: A Sharply Divided Society on the Brink of a Cultural Civil War*, Washington Report on Middle East Affairs, (July/August 1999), *at* www.wrmea.com/backissues/0799/9907086.html.

22   Allan C. Brownfeld, *Growth of Religious Extremism in Israel Threatens the Peace Process*, August/September 2000, *available at* http://www.washington-report.org/archives/Aug_Sept_2000/0010072.html.

23   *Id.*

24   *See* Allan C. Brownfeld, *Murder in the Name of God: Where Religious Extremism Can Lead*, at http://www.againstbombing.com/Rabinmurder.htm.

25   Hashavna (*The Weekly*), November 3, 1995.

his thoughts, and scatter his mind that he may steadily diminish until he reaches his death."[26] As Eskin chanted, the other rabbis joined in, saying, "Put to death the cursed Yitzhak, son of Rosa Rabin, as quickly as possible because of his hatred for the Chosen People."[27] The ceremony came to an end with Eskin shouting, "May you be damned, damned, damned!"[28]

In the aftermath of Rabin's assassination, the State Attorney General, Michael Ben-Yair, chose not to press charges against rabbis who had openly incited against Rabin. The most obvious question is why? Did Michael Ben-Yair exercise legitimate prosecutorial discretion, or did the Attorney General grant religious speech immunity? In a private conversation with a former minister in Rabin's government,[29] the latter suggested that Ben-Yair was "afraid" to act against the rabbis due to concern as to how their congregants would respond. Did all rabbis in Israel incite violence against Rabin in 1995? Of course not. Not all Orthodox rabbis incited violence. Nor were they the only group in Israel stirring up the political climate. Yet it must be noted in no uncertain terms—*the most vociferous inciters against Rabin were rabbis.*

In the aftermath of Rabin's assassination, the general impression among the Israeli public was that rabbis had been granted immunity with respect to their words spoken prior to the assassination. One of the clear lessons learned is the extraordinary personal security extended today to the Israeli Prime Minster. The irony must not be lost, however: the security model regarding how to protect an Israeli Prime Minister was fundamentally changed in response to extreme Jewish religious terrorism, not Palestinian terrorism. In 2004, as Ariel Sharon called for a Knesset vote whether to pull out of Gaza, security increased around the Prime Minister as another assassination was feared. The late Tommy Lapid, then Justice Minister, said that statements by right-wing rabbis opposed to the evacuation plan could incite violence among Orthodox Jews, and warned

---

26   Michael Karpin & Ina Friedman, *Murder in the Name of God: The Plot to Kill Yitzhak Rabin* 90–91 (Metropolitan Books, 1998).

27   *Id.*

28   Zion Zohar, *Pulsa De-Nura: The Innovation of Modern Magic and Ritual,* 27 Modern Judaism 1, 72 (2007).

29   Name withheld at my discretion; content and date of discussion in my records.

that "after the Rabin murder, we must observe the boundary between acceptable and criminal statements."[30]

Further complicating this issue is that some of the most prominent rabbis involved have denied that their words should be considered as anything more than just that—words. Rabbi Abraham Hecht, president of the Rabbinical Alliance of America and considered by many as one of America's most articulate Orthodox leaders, noted that he "made a mistake" by engaging in what he termed a theoretical debate about Jewish law and West Bank settlers, but insists that the intent of his words has been distorted. At a conference of 1,500 Israeli rabbis in Manhattan, months before the assassination, Hecht cited the teachings of Maimonides and asserted that the punishment for endangering Jewish lives or divinely ordained property was death. Hecht insisted he never spoke directly about Rabin, and noted that he sent an apology letter to Rabin two weeks prior to the assassination, apologizing for any words that "have caused hurt." Hecht also denied that his speeches or articles could have been what pushed Amir to murder, given they were stated and published in New York and in English. Hecht did, however, acknowledge that his comments at the conference were a "mistake" and contributed to a "shrill" debate.[31]

Assuming that Hecht's evaluation of his own statements is accurate, the next question is obvious—*should* he have known that his words could be used to justify violence? And if so, did his reckless disregard for that possibility subject him to criminal or civil liability for his words? While these are rhetorical questions their significance should not be lost looking ahead. Hindsight is always 20-20 vision, and had Rabin not been assassinated, it is very likely we would consider Hecht's words to be part of the marketplace of ideas, albeit unpleasant.

---

30   Ian MacKinnon, *Rabbis 'incite violence' over Gaza plan*, TIMES ONLINE, October 22, 2004. *Available at* http://www.timesonline.co.uk/tol/news/world/article497358.ece.

31   Joe Sexton, *How a Rabbi's Rhetoric Did, or Didn't, Justify Assassination*. The New York Times, December 3, 1995. Interestingly, Hecht would be later cited by another would-be assassin, Harry Shapiro. In 1997, Shapiro pleaded guilty to federal charges that he had planted a pipe bomb in a Florida synagogue to prevent Shimon Peres from speaking there in support of the Oslo Accords. *See* Allan C. Brownfeld, *Extremism in Israel is Fueled by a Growing Ultra-Orthodox Movement in the U.S.*, Washington Report on Middle East Affairs, December 2000, pp. 71–72. *Available at* http://www.washington-report.org/archives/Jan_Feb_2001/0101071.html.

WHAT COULD ISRAEL HAVE DONE DIFFERENTLY?

The even more difficult question is what Israeli authorities should have done *prior* to the assassination. Today, many would agree that the rabbis who made the most inflammatory and pointed statements against Rabin should have been held legally accountable for their words. That said, it is important to note the extraordinarily broad freedom of speech standard advanced by Israeli liberals and conservatives alike. While many politicians and academics called on Ben-Yair to prosecute the inciting rabbis, his decision not to do so was met with praise amongst those who favor an expansive definition of freedom of speech. Should the Israeli government have acted to stop the religious extremist leaders from making their statements at all? If Israel had tried to quell criminal speech before the assassination, would it have succeeded or merely resulted in even more hateful words being spoken in less public places?

The question is asked in the context of a conceivable peace process with the Palestinian Authority resulting in bilateral disengagement from the West Bank. If an Israeli government, regardless of political party and Prime Minister, decides to dismantle the settlements, violence will be all but inevitable. The violence, largely pitting extremist Jewish settlers against soldiers, would be primarily driven by religious extremism.

Whether it is solely religious or a confluence of Messianic religious nationalism, the critical issue is whether rabbis, predicated on their understanding of the Old Testament, will preach that disengagement must be physically resisted. The fear, based on undeniable historical precedent, is that one of the followers will take these teachings to their conclusion—that a Prime Minister who decides on such a course is a traitor.

According to Ministry of Justice Prosecutorial Regulations,[32] the principle of freedom of speech is a fundamental underpinning of the State of Israel. The decision to file an indictment regarding freedom of speech requires balancing state security and public order with the right to freedom of speech and association. While laudable in proposing lofty goals and policy, it begs the question of whether the scales are tipped too heavily in favor of individual freedom at the expense of individual safety and public security.

---

32   *Available at* http://www.justice.gov.il/NR/rdonlyres/DED2D846-34F4-4CFC-8F97-1C5324C111AD/0/211.pdf, last viewed June 19, 2008.

Even the most liberal democracies have set certain limits on freedom of speech, but those limits still allow for a broad speech standard. Both the U.S. Supreme Court in *R.A.V. v. City of Saint Paul*,[33] which limited only the most heinous hate speech, and the European Court on Human Rights in *Lingens v. Austria*,[34] which insisted that Austria expand its law concerning acceptable freedom of expression to match Article 10 of the European Convention of Human Rights,[35] established an extremely broad freedom of speech standard. While these standards allow free expression to flourish, they may need to be restricted to protect national security given the danger posed by religious extremism.

If rabbis were to once again issue a *pulsa denura* against an Israeli prime minister,[36] then imposing limits on speech would seem to be the appropriate, if not practical, response. However, imposing limits is but the first step. Un-enforced laws are more problematic than failure to legislate; the latter represents political considerations whereas the former manifests institutional weakness and an unwillingness to confront sensitive matters.

THE PROPOSED TEST

In the context of identifying religious extremism as *the* threat that most endangers contemporary democratic society, the challenge is how we

---

33 *R.A.V. v. City of Saint Paul, Minn.*, 505 U.S. 377 (1992). Petitioner burnt a cross in the yard of an African-American family; after his arrest, he argued that 'hate speech' was protected by the First Amendment. This case held that government has the right to limit freedom of speech under the "fighting words" doctrine as long as the ordinance does not prohibit otherwise permitted speech solely on the basis of the subjects the speech addresses; in this case the ordinance was ruled to be to restrictive.

34 *Lingens v. Austria*, 8 EHRR 407 (1986). Applicant, the publisher of a magazine which printed articles critical of the Austrian Chancellor appealed Austrian ruling which fined him and confiscated his magazines; the European Court overturned the ruling, citing Article 10 of the European Convention allowing for most forms of free expression.

35 European Convention on Human Rights Article 10.

36 Former Prime Minister Sharon, before the disengagement from the Gaza Strip, was subjected to this "curse". The nationalist-religious political parties and rabbis relationship with Sharon was complicated—on the one hand, he was the primary architect of the Jewish settlements in the West Bank and Gaza Strip; on the other hand, he dismantled (there are various theories as to his motivation/s) the settlements in the Gaza Strip.

square the constitutional right to practice religion with the concept that religious extremism can constitute such a threat. While "clear and present danger" is the American paradigm for determining when words constitute incitement, religious extremism forces us to ask the following question: Should the *Brandenburg*[37] test be re-articulated, or even over-ruled?

Brandenburg v. Ohio, 395 U.S. 444 (1969)

Brandenburg is one of the most speech-protective cases in American jurisprudence. A leader of the Ku Klux Klan was convicted of advocating violence under Ohio State law after participating in a KKK rally. The U.S. Supreme Court reversed the conviction, holding that government cannot, under the First Amendment, punish the abstract advocacy of violence.

Under *Brandenburg*, the government can only limit speech if the speech:

1. Promotes imminent harm;

2. There is a high likelihood that the speech will result in listeners participating in illegal action; and

3. The speaker intended to cause such illegality.

This test, while extremely protective of freedom of speech, does not adequately address the *potential* danger posed by a pastor who weekly preaches hellfire against physicians who perform abortions. How is a police officer supposed to know that such a sermon is meant rhetorically and therefore fails the third element? How is a police officer to know whether there is a high likelihood that a congregant will act on such a sermon? And as the sermons occur weekly, when does the harm they promote become "imminent"?

Contemporary religious extremism leaves decision-makers and the public alike with no choice but to re-contour constitutionally granted rights as they pertain to religion and speech. The question is one of line-drawing. It is easy to state that religious extremism needs to be limited. Many in the five surveyed nations would concur with that thesis; the challenge is in clearly, precisely, and concisely drawing that line.

If *Brandenburg* is to be re-fashioned, a clear, workable test must be established in the alternative. States cannot engage in case-by-case analysis in determining when religious liberties are to be limited. Amorphous criteria both invite governmental excess and create due process problems

---

37   395 U.S. 444 (1969).

as the person of faith will not be able to predict whether his or her actions conform to the law. Therefore, I propose three possibilities:

1. **Unprotected speech**—Categorizing religious speech that promotes hatred or violence of others as wholly unprotected incitement, without the need for determining intent or for ascertaining whether the speech likely resulted in illegality. In other words, this approach would apply only the first element of the Brandenburg test and remove the last two;

2. **Lower Intent**—Lowering the bar for the intent element of the *Brandenburg* test whenever the speaker in question is a figure of religious authority; or

3. **Intermediate Scrutiny**—Leaving the three *Brandenburg* elements as they are, but lowering the standard from traditional strict scrutiny to intermediate scrutiny in the case of extremist religious speech.

EXTREMIST RELIGIOUS SPEECH AS "UNPROTECTED SPEECH"

The first option redefines the extremist speech in question as unprotected. Drawing the line between protected and unprotected speech is precisely what Courts in the United States have done in cases involving obscenity, libel, and incitement.[38] In *Chaplinsky v. New Hampshire*,[39] the Supreme Court held that statutes that prohibit "fighting words" do not violate the First Amendment when the speech is likely to cause a violent response in the listener. Fighting words are also unprotected when they cause clear and present danger of a riot, disorder, or other threat to public safety that the police will be unable to prevent.[40]

Courts have also held that defendants can be held civilly liable for physical injury caused by their words. In *Weirum v. RKO General, Inc.*,[41] decided well after *Chaplinsky*, the Supreme Court of California affirmed an award of damages against a radio station that held a contest where drivers sped throughout the listening area, racing to be the first to find a traveling radio disc jockey. Two minors, driving in separate cars, forced another car off the road in their pursuit. The driver of that car was killed,

---

38   For a greater discussion of First Amendment case law, see the Appendix.

39   315 U.S. 568 (1942).

40   *Feiner v. New York*, 340 US 315 (1951).

41   15 Cal. 3d 40 (1975).

and his wife and children sued the radio station. The Court rejected the radio station's First Amendment defense, noting that the broadcasts repeatedly encouraged listeners to speed to announced locations and act in inherently dangerous ways. "The First Amendment does not sanction the infliction of physical injury merely because it is achieved by word, rather than act."[42]

Could similar analyses apply to the statements of Israeli rabbis described earlier? In *Rice v. Paladin Enterprises*,[43] the U.S. District Court for the District of Maryland and the Fourth Circuit Court of Appeals grappled with this question, coming to two different results. In *Paladin*, plaintiffs filed a wrongful death action against a publishing company that had produced books called *Hit Man: A Technical Manual for Independent Contractors* and *How to Make a Disposable Silencer, Vol. II*. These books were used by James Perry to prepare for the murder of Mildred Horn, her eight-year-old quadriplegic son Trevor and Trevor's nurse, Janice Saunders.[44] Perry acted as a "contract killer," hired by Mildred's ex-husband Lawrence Horn, who wanted to collect the $2 million that his son Trevor held in trust after the accident that left him paralyzed for life.

Paladin moved for summary judgment, arguing that the publication of the two books was protected under the First Amendment. The District Court agreed, stating that while the content of *Hit Man* is "enough to engender nausea," it did not fall into one of the categories of unprotected speech. The District Court noted that *Brandenburg* laid out the standard for incitement cases, and concluded the Paladin books did not meet the test. Noting the difference between "advocacy" and "incitement," the District Court held that the books merely teach how to implement a successful murder-for-hire and do not "cross that line between permissible advocacy and impermissible incitation to crime or violence" by encouraging anyone to commit murder.[45]

---

42   *Weirum v. RKO General, Inc.*, 15 Cal. 3d 40, 48 (1975).

43   128 F.3d 233 (4th Cir. 1997).

44   After the Fourth Circuit overturned the District Court's ruling of summary judgment for the publisher, the United States Supreme Court denied certiorari. Paladin settled the case with the victim's families for an undisclosed amount of money.

45   *Rice v. Paladin Enterprises, Inc.*, 128 F.3d 233, 263 (4th Cir. 1997).

On appeal, the Fourth Circuit rejected Paladin's arguments, holding that the books' only purposes were to assist criminals in preparation of murder, and as such did not merit the First Amendment's protection of "mere advocacy."[46] Quoting from the books at length, the Court noted that *Hit Man* and *Silencers* instructed contract killers in how to negotiate with clients, request "expense money" up front, select a location for the murder, use a rental car to reach the victim's location, establish a "base" at a motel close to the "jobsite," use an AR-7 rifle when starting out and drill out the serial numbers on the rifle.[47] This level of detailed instruction, in combination with the fact that Perry had followed the instructions to the letter, led the Court of Appeals to conclude that the books could not be considered anything other than unprotected incitement.

If the Fourth Circuit's view in *Paladin* is applied to religious extremist speech, speech which serves no purpose other than to endorse violent action on religious grounds, it may be appropriately considered "unprotected" under the First Amendment. This approach would allow governments and private actors to apply criminal and civil liability against religious speakers such as the rabbis discussed previously. It may also allow governments to attempt to impose a prior restraint on speakers known previously to have crossed the line between advocacy and incitement.

LOWERING THE INTENT ELEMENT IN *BRANDENBURG*

The second alternative is to lower the intent element in the *Brandenburg* test whenever the speaker is an individual with religious authority. In *Brandenberg*, the Court held that "the constitutional guarantees of free speech and free press do not permit a state to forbid or proscribe advocacy of the use of force or of law violation except where such advocacy is directed to inciting or producing imminent lawless action and is likely to incite or produce such action."[48] The court went on to say, "'The mere abstract teaching of the moral propriety or even moral necessity for a resort to force and violence, is not the same as preparing a group for violent action and steeling it to such action."[49]

---

46   *Id.* at 245.

47   *Id.* at 239–40.

48   *Brandenberg v. Ohio*, 395 U.S. 444, 447 (1969).

49   *Id.* at 448.

As mentioned in the introduction, the authority and power of an extremist religious cleric is potentially extraordinary. Therefore, when we examine the three prongs of the *Brandenburg* test—imminence, likelihood, intent—the first two are almost certainly met in the case of an extremist religious authority determined to encourage his congregation to act. Sermons regularly addressing various dangers and evils will ultimately reach a "critical mass" and the listener's violent act will become imminent. A listener is likely to obey the words of an individual he or she views as an ultimate authority on spiritual matters.

The final question is that of determining the speaker's intent. As illustrated by the example of Yitzhak Rabin and Rabbi Hecht, this can be a difficult task. In an interview with *New York Magazine* prior to the assassination, Rabbi Hecht stated that Jewish law "says very clearly, if a man kills [someone who endangers Jewish lives or land], he has done a good deed."[50] To one reader, it is obvious that Hecht was instructing followers to kill Rabin; to others, the statement remains a mere theory. Hecht himself has insisted that his intent was never to provoke violence.

Therefore, would it be prudent to consider whether the third element of the *Brandenburg* test should be relaxed when the speaker in question is a figure of religious authority? Such figures should be on constructive notice that their followers are even more likely to act on their directives, and that such an action is more imminent by virtue of it being heard repeatedly. It is reasonable to demand that such speakers make absolutely clear their intent when speaking on matters that could result in violence to others, and not speak in couched terms and subtext to muddle the intent analysis. In reality, speakers in positions of religious authority are already on constructive notice that their words are taken seriously by their listeners. After all, the trust and confidence given to religious leaders was illustrated in a recent poll in the U.S.: 85 percent of Americans trust clergymen, while only 44 percent trust a TV newscaster.[51]

---

50   R.I. Freidman, *The Rabbi who Sentenced Yitzhak Rabin to Death*, NEW YORK MAGAZINE, Oct. 9, 1995, at 24.

51   *See* Harris Poll #62, November 11, 1998: Over 85 percent of people say they trust clergymen and priests at www.harrisinteractive.com/harris_poll/index.asp?PID=145.

INTERMEDIATE SCRUTINY VS. STRICT SCRUTINY

The final option is to lower the Constitutional standard (for the analysis of extremist religious speech) from strict scrutiny to intermediate scrutiny. When examining regulations on the content of speech, the Supreme Court has used strict scrutiny; when examining regulations on content-neutral regulations, it has applied intermediate scrutiny.[52] The more important and fundamental the liberty interest involved, the more likely it is that the Court will use the most exacting level of scrutiny. Strict scrutiny requires that the government show a compelling interest to justify the proposed law, and that the proposed law is narrowly tailored to the problem it addresses. Intermediate scrutiny requires that the government show an important interest, and that its proposed law substantially fits the problem addressed.[53]

Religious speech is different than secular speech for one major reason: God is the subject and or object of the speech. A member of the clergy is generally perceived by congregants to be the recognized interpreter of how God intends the individual to act. While different congregations may have different ideas regarding the power and status of clergy, all believe that their clergy possess certain qualifications and characteristics relevant to religious leadership. Therefore, while freedom of speech is a hallowed principle of liberal democracy, that principle requires a distinction between secular speech and clerical speech.

Distinguishing between the two categories is admittedly a problematic concept. The U.S. Supreme Court addressed this concept in *Cantwell v. Connecticut*, ruling that the First Amendment's protection of religious freedom "embraces two concepts—the freedom to believe and the freedom to act. The first is absolute but, in the nature of things, the second cannot be. Conduct remains subject to regulation for the protection of society."[54] In suggesting that clergy are to be held to a higher standard

---

52 *Turner Broadcasting System Inc. v. Federal Communication Commission*, 520 U.S. 180 (1997): "Most exacting scrutiny to regulations that suppress, disadvantage, or impose differential burdens upon speech because of it's content." "Regulations that are unrelated to the content of speech are subject to an intermediate level of scrutiny because in most cases they pose a less substantial risk of excising certain ideas or viewpoints from the public dialogue."

53 For further discussion of the three levels of scrutiny in U.S. Constitutional analysis, see the Appendix.

54 *Cantwell v. Connecticut*, 310 US 296, 303–304 (1940).

with respect to freedom of speech, a distinction must be drawn between "extremist clergy" and mainstream faith leaders. If this distinction were to be implemented, would it constitute discrimination? In the American constitutional paradigm, the distinction is subject to attack on both Equal Protection Clause[55] and Due Process Clause[56] grounds.

This is precisely the critical dilemma and extraordinary danger. By identifying religious extremism as *the* contemporary danger to civil, democratic society, the appropriate follow-up question is whether this proposed test impermissibly discriminates against a specific class and restricts only their speech. While extreme religious inciters are the primary problem, they are not the only concern facing society. Though the practical result of the proposed approach may be prosecution of religious inciters, the requisite legislation must not be structured in a category-specific manner. By expanding *Brandenburg* to include all speech, not just one category of speech, inciters of all kinds would be subject to criminal prosecution. In the context of religious-based incitement, the speech would not be protected.

WHEN TO LIMIT?

Having established that religious speech that incites followers to violence should enjoy a lower standard of protection than other speech, we now come to the question—should governments merely punish speakers after their words provoke violence, or should they step in once the objectionable words have been spoken? After all, if the goal is to protect other members of society, will punishing speakers *after* violence has occurred be deterrent enough? Clearly not. Given that what makes religious speakers so dangerous is that they repeat their messages on a weekly basis, the government needs to step in *as soon as* the religious speaker makes his or her first statement inciting to violence, thereby preventing future statements.

One commentator has described this proposal of limiting clerical right to free speech as "paradoxical."[57] Without passing judgment on the proposal, he commented, "it turns free speech thinking upside down." Another reader noted that we usually think of the freedom of clergy to

---

55   U.S. Const. art. I.

56   *Id.*

57   E-mail correspondence, June 19, 2008 (email in author's records).

preach as among the *most* protected speech, not the *least* protected speech.[58]

Yet the fundamental basis for this proposal is that the threat posed by religious speech as manifested by *pulsa denura* should not be protected as freedom of expression. The United States and other countries already recognize the illegality of incitement. This proposal merely adds that limits be imposed on free speech *before* someone acts on that speech, predicated on the possibility that someone *may* act. This restraint is admittedly problematic for at its core the proposal recommends restricting speech *earlier* than existing case law and legislation in liberal, civil democracies presently mandate.[59] While the liberal, democratic ethos advocates maximum rights of and for the individual, the contemporary manifestation of extreme religious belief requires reexamining that premise. The burden is convincing the reader *both* as to the necessity of limiting otherwise protected rights and creating a road map for decision makers and the public to do so.

THE NETHERLANDS: RELIGIOUS VS. SECULAR SPEECH AND THEO VAN GOGH

How does one describe Theo van Gogh? A week in the Netherlands, meeting and speaking with a wide array of reporters, academics, politicians, security officials, and filmmakers, left me with numerous visions of who and what Theo van Gogh was. Clearly, Theo van Gogh was a filmmaker, actor, and columnist well known for his open criticism of Islam, murdered after the release of his anti-Islam film, *Submission*. The two most striking descriptions are provocateur and gadfly. There is little doubt that Van Gogh irritated, enraged, and offended a wide array of people from different ethnic and religious groups, particularly Muslims. It is also fair to say, based on interviews with people who knew him, that the fact that he offended others was of little concern to him. While clearly offensive to many and irritating to others, Van Gogh represented an important aspect of liberal democracy—the right to speak, the right to create and the right to express an opinion, even if considered outrageous. It was this quality that led to his brutal murder.

---

58   Private conversation with the author; identity known to author.

59   *See Ashcroft v. American Civil Liberties Union*, 535 U.S. 564 (2002); *Center for Individual Freedom v. Carmouche*, 449 F.3d 655 (5th Circuit 2006); *Brandenberg v. Ohio* 395 U.S. 444 (1969).

On November 2, 2004, Mohammed Bouyeri shot Van Gogh eight times, slit his throat, nearly decapitating him, and stabbed him in the chest. Two knives were left in Van Gogh's corpse, one attaching a five-page "open letter to Hirshi Ali" (sic, Hirsi Ali) to his body that threatened Western governments, Jews, and Van Gogh's collaborator, Ayaan Hirsi Ali. Bouyeri was convicted and sentenced to life in prison with no chance of parole.

Bouyeri was a member of the Hofstad Network, which the Dutch government characterizes as a terrorist organization.[60] The Hofstad Network is influenced by the ideology of Takfir wal-Hijra, a Muslim extremist group which advocates armed battle against Jews, Christians, and apostate Muslims in order to restore an Islamic world order. Takfir wal-Hijra's ideology instructs that the ends justify the means; group members adopt non-Islamic appearances and practices (shaving their beards, wearing ties, drinking alcohol, eating pork) in order to blend in with non-Muslims.[61] The Hofstad Group has been suspected of planning to kill several members of the Dutch government and parliament.

What differentiates the Hofstad Network from Theo van Gogh, who openly espoused highly controversial views in the media? If both Hofstad and Van Gogh have the potential to incite, if they both have the potential to persuade people to act on their behalf, should not they both be subject to similar limitations? After all, it is a matter of perspective in determining whose ideas are more offensive when in theoretical form only. The difference is that extremist religious speech more readily instigates violence than secular speech does.

Van Gogh was a powerful voice for some, a gadfly for others, dismissed in some quarters as a racist not to be taken seriously and considered by some an unrepentant Islam basher who must be silenced. But, if the ultimate strength of liberal democracy is the voice that makes us uncomfortable—right or left, religious or secular—then Van Gogh manifests that strength. Was he extreme in his views? According to many with whom I met, the answer is yes. But, those views in the context of the

---

60   On January 23, 2008, a Dutch Appeals Court ruled that the government did not meet its burden of proving that the Hofstad Group is a terrorist organization as defined by Dutch law.

61   Transcript, *Al Qaeda's New Front*, produced & directed by Neil Docherty, Frontline, *available at* http://www.pbs.org/wgbh/pages/frontline/shows/front/etc/script.html.

right to free speech did not fall into the category of words that need to be silenced. The right to free speech was, in some ways, designed for a Theo van Gogh. He was not a spiritual leader; he had no army of followers who were going to endanger either national security or public order. While offensive to some, he was not a danger to society at large or to specific elements of society.

Therein lies the most significant difference between religious speech and secular speech in the current paradigm facing liberal democracies. Extreme religious speech *does* present a threat, or at least has the potential to present a threat in a manner that secular speech today does not. That is why limits on free speech do not pertain to a Theo van Gogh, but do apply to rabbis, pastors, and imams who espouse extreme views that threaten specific individuals and larger communities alike.

EXAMINING TURKEY: WHEN CAN A STATE APPLY LIMITS?

Applying limits to speech is a balancing act between an individual's rights and the duty a state has to protect its citizens. Turkey has implemented this balancing act directly into its constitution. The Constitution of the Republic of Turkey lays out the fundamental rights and freedoms of the Turkish citizens:

> Everyone possesses inherent fundamental rights and freedoms which are inviolable and inalienable. The fundamental rights and freedoms also comprise the duties and responsibilities of the individual to the society, his or her family, and other individuals."[62] Further, the Constitution explains how these "inherent" and "fundamental" freedoms must be protected, limiting the method and ability of restricting those rights. "Fundamental rights and freedoms may be restricted only by law and in conformity with the reasons mentioned in the relevant articles of the Constitution without infringing upon their essence. These restrictions shall not be in conflict with the letter and spirit of the Constitution and the requirements of the democratic order of the society and the secular Republic and the principle of proportionality.[63]

As an example of a fundamental freedom, the Constitution notes, "everyone has the right to freedom of thought and opinion. No one shall be compelled to reveal his thoughts and opinions for any reason or purpose,

---

62   CONSTITUTION OF TURKEY, Article 12 (2001).

63   CONSTITUTION OF TURKEY, Article 13 (2001).

nor shall anyone be blamed or accused on account of his thoughts and opinions."[64]

With respect to speech, the Constitution states that the freedom of speech is fundamental.

> Everyone has the right to express and disseminate his thoughts and opinion by speech, in writing or in pictures or through other media, individually or collectively. This right includes the freedom to receive and impart information and ideas without interference from official authorities. This provision shall not preclude subjecting transmission by radio, television, cinema, and similar means to a system of licensing.[65]

However, the Constitution is explicit that the freedom of speech is not absolute, and can legally be restricted.

> The exercise of these freedoms may be restricted for the purposes of protecting national security, public order and public safety, the basic characteristics of the Republic and safeguarding the indivisible integrity of the State with its territory and nation, preventing crime, punishing offenders, withholding information duly classified as a state secret, protecting the reputation and rights and private and family life of others, or protecting professional secrets as prescribed by law, or ensuring the proper functioning of the judiciary.

> The formalities, conditions and procedures to be applied in exercising the right to expression and dissemination of thought shall be prescribed by law.[66]

Religious leaders are also subject to strict limitations on their freedom of speech. "Article 219 of the Penal Code prohibits imams, priests, rabbis, or other religious leaders from 'reproaching or vilifying' the Government or the laws of the state while performing their duties. Violations are punishable by prison terms of 1 month to 1 year, or 3 months to 2 years if the crime involves inciting others to disobey the law."[67]

---

64   CONSTITUTION OF TURKEY, Article 25 (2001).

65   CONSTITUTION OF TURKEY, Article 26 (2001).

66   *Id.*

67   *Turkey: International Religious Freedom Report, 2008*, Bureau of Democracy, Human Rights and Labor, Department of the State, September 19, 2008, *available at* http://www.state.gov/g/drl/rls/irf/2008/108476.htm, last visited October 6, 2008.

Religious leaders can also be charged with incitement. For example, a "Syriac priest in Diyarbakir was briefly detained in December 2000, put on trial, but acquitted in April 2001 of charges that he 'incited ethnic hatred' by stating in October 2000 that allegations of 'Armenian genocide' during World War I were justified."[68] In May of 2001, Mehment Kutlular, an Islamic leader of the Nur Cemaati religious community "began serving a 2-year sentence for 'inciting religious hatred' when he published a statement in October 1999 alleging that the August 1999 earthquake (that killed over 17,000 people) was 'divine retribution' for laws banning headscarves in state buildings and universities."[69]

In Turkey, the tension between free exercise of religion and the secular state is defined in, and resolved in, the Constitution. The Turkish Constitution provides for a freedom of religious belief[70] and a freedom of religious practice[71] so long as[72] those practices do not hinder the integrity and existence of the secular state.[73] The Constitution gives the state a right to curtail these "fundamental rights" in the name of the secular state. For example, "the Government imposes limitations on Islamic and other religious groups and significant restrictions on Islamic religious expression in government offices and state-run institutions, including universities, for the stated reason of preserving the 'secular

---

68 *Turkey: International Religious Freedom Report, 2001*, Bureau of Democracy, Human Rights and Labor, Department of the State, October 26, 2001, *available at* http://www.state.gov/g/drl/rls/irf/2001/5694.htm, last visited October 6, 2008.

69 *Id.*

70 Constitution of Turkey, Article 24, Freedom of Religion and Conscience (stating "Everyone has the right to freedom of conscience, religious belief and conviction.").

71 Constitution of Turkey, Article 24, Freedom of Religion and Conscience (stating "Acts of worship, religious services, and ceremonies shall be conducted freely, provided that they do not violate the provisions of Article 14).

72 Constitution of Turkey, Article 24, Freedom of Religion and Conscience (stating "Acts of worship, religious services, and ceremonies shall be conducted freely, Acts of worship, religious services, and ceremonies shall be conducted freely, provided that they do not violate the provisions of Article 14).

73 Constitution of Turkey, Article 14, Prohibition of Abuse of Fundamental Rights and Freedoms; *see also Turkey: International Religious Freedom Report, 2008*, Bureau of Democracy, Human Rights and Labor, Department of the State, September 19, 2008, *available at* http://www.state.gov/g/drl/rls/irf/2008/108476.htm, last visited October 6, 2008.

state.'"[74] The constitution states that "[n]one of the rights and freedoms embodied in the Constitution shall be exercised with the aim of violating the indivisible integrity of the state with its territory and nation, and endangering the existence of the democratic and secular order of the Turkish Republic based upon human rights."[75] For Turkey, therefore, while there is a tension between freedom and the secular state, the constitution intends for the secular state to remain supreme.

Turkey has come under fire for excessively limiting free expression. The balance between protecting the security of a nation and violating the rights of citizens is a continual struggle, both in Turkey and in other countries throughout the world. The Turkish Human Rights Foundation has identified 14 parts of the Turkish Code that potentially restrict free expression.[76] In particular, critics focus on Article 301,[77] which makes it

---

74   *Turkey: International Religious Freedom Report, 2008*, Bureau of Democracy, Human Rights and Labor, Department of the State, September 19, 2008, *available at* http://www.state.gov/g/drl/rls/irf/2008/108476.htm, last visited October 6, 2008.

75   CONSTITUTION OF TURKEY, Article 14, Prohibition of Abuse of Fundamental Rights and Freedoms.

76   The lists consists of the following: Article 84 – regulating encouraging and aiding suicide; Article 125 on denigrating honor, dignity and esteem and insulting a public official; Article 132 – regulating violation of privacy of communication; Article 134 – regulating privacy of personal life; Article 215 – regulating praise of crime and criminal; Article 216 – regulating incitement of hatred and enmity; Article 218 – on crimes committed against public peace through the press; Article 285 – regulating violation of confidentiality of investigation; Article 286 – regulating audio and visual recording of the proceedings of investigation and prosecution; Article 288 – on attempts to influence fair trial; Article 299 – on the crime of insulting the president; Article 301 – on insulting Turkishness, the republic and the organs and institutions of the state; Article 305 – regulating activities against fundamental national interests; Article 318 – regulating the crime of discouraging people from military service. *See* Göksel Bozkurt, *Turkey debates free expression of thought*, TURKISH DAILY NEWS, October 1, 2006.

77   "How much progress can a society, containing intellectuals, artists, writers and caricaturists that are unable to express themselves, achieve? Don't people living in Turkey deserve the right to think and freely express what they think? Novelist Elif Şafak, who was tried and speedily acquitted in a case under Article 301, says freedom of expression must exist in Turkey not because somebody wants us to have it but for our own people. What can a writer produce if they can't express what they can imagine? If they do manage to produce something, who would like it? Can thought be restricted? Should non-violent thought and its expression be free? How far are the Turkish people free to think and express their thoughts? Who

a crime to denigrate "Turkishness," the Republic of Turkey, the judiciary, the military, or the judiciary. [78]

Many newspapers and press organizations fear that the revised law remains sufficiently vague to allow for arbitrary prosecutions and court decisions, chilling freedom of expression.[79] To date, several journalists and writers have been prosecuted under Article 301. Elif Şafak was prosecuted under Article 301 for "insulting Turkishness" in her novel *The Bastards of Istanbul*.[80] The 2006 Nobel literature laureate, Orhan Pamuk, was tried under Article 301, mainly for contesting the official "line" on the Ottoman massacres of Armenians, which many countries have recognized as genocide.[81] Finally, "Publisher Erol Karaaslan said he would be questioned by an Istanbul prosecutor on Wednesday as part of the official investigation into [Richard] Dawkins' book, *The God Delusion*."[82]

---

will draw the boundaries? Would the Republic of Turkey be harmed if freedom of expression was fully ensured? Would the integrity of the state be endangered then? These are the questions that surround the Article 301 controversy in Turkey." Göksel Bozkurt, Turkey debates free expression of thought, TURKISH DAILY NEWS, October 1, 2006.

78 Penal Code, Republic of Turkey, Article 301 (2005):

To Denigrate Turkishness, Republic, and Institutions and Organs of Article 301:
"1 - A person who publicly denigrates Turkishness, the Republic or the Grand National Assembly of Turkey, shall be punishable by imprisonment of between six months and three years.
2 - A person who publicly denigrates Government of the Republic of Turkey, the judicial institutions of the State, the military or security organizations shall be punishable by imprisonment of between six months and two years.
3 - In cases where denigration of Turkishness is committed by a Turkish citizen in another country the punishment shall be increased by one third.
4 - Expression of thought intended to criticize shall not constitute crime."

79 "Turkey's New Penal Code Touches Raw Nerves," EURACTIV, June 2, 2005, *available at* http://www.euractiv.com/en/enlargement/turkey-new-penal-code-touches-raw-nerves/article-140266.

80 A judge ruled that the evidence was not substantiated. Göksel Bozkurt, Turkey debates free expression of thought, TURKISH DAILY NEWS, October 1, 2006.

81 *Available at* http://www.eubusiness.com/Turkey/1194378422.71/.

82 *Available at* http://edition.cnn.com/2007/WORLD/europe/11/28fdawkins.turkey.ap2findex.html.

Turkey is struggling with a more immediate threat of religious violence than is the U.S. The somewhat severe limitations that Turkey has placed on religious practice must be understood in the context of that struggle. Although the Turkish ban on headscarves should not serve as a model, the benefits of Turkey's secularism should inspire other countries to combat extremism with less fear of offending religious groups.

GREAT BRITAIN: ENDING A LONG HISTORY OF TOLERANCE?

The UK historically has practiced extraordinary tolerance for free speech. In the context of the freedom of religious speech, that tolerance is based in part on the historically limited influence of the Anglican Church[83] in English life. Great Britain's commitment to freedom of speech predates modern international conventions. British writer and philosopher John Milton was one of the earliest proponents of freedom of expression, and Sir Thomas More helped establish the parliamentary privilege of free speech during the 1500s.[84] In the 1600s, Milton argued that censorship acts to the detriment of a nation's progress, since truth will always defeat falsehood; but a single individual cannot be trusted to tell the two apart, and therefore no individual can be trusted to act as censor for all individuals.[85] John Stuart Mill furthered Milton's arguments in the 1800s by promoting the principle of the "marketplace of ideas," where objectionable speech has a place since truth will prevail, and even hateful speech has a value in that it provides an opportunity for others to confront opposition, examine their assumptions, and ultimately refine their own thoughts and arguments.[86]

In recent years, homegrown Islamic terrorist attacks, influenced by al Qaeda but ultimately separate from the organization, have rocked the social fabric in Great Britain. On July 7, 2005, 56 people were killed in a

---

83   *See* U.S. Department of State, http://www.state.gov/g/drl/rls/irf/2006/71416. htm. *See generally* Peter Cumper, *The United Kingdom and the UN Declaration on the Elimination of Intolerance*, 21 EMORY INTL L. REV. 13.

84   *The Life of Sir Thomas More, available at* http://www.luminarium.org/renlit/ morebio.htm. *See also* Parliamentary Privilege and Free Speech: MPs' privileges and citizens' freedom from oppression, March 9, 2006, *available at* www.adls. org.nz/filedownload?id=b3e74fd4-6cb8-4276-9029-a15a59247246.

85   John Milton, *Areopagitica*, 1643.

86   John Stuart Mill, *On Liberty*, 1859.

series of bombings in the London subway.[87] In August 2006, a plot to simultaneously destroy U.S.-bound commercial airlines departing from London was uncovered;[88] on June 30, 2007, Glasgow Airport was attacked.[89]

In the attacks' aftermath, the British Parliament passed counterterrorism-related legislation. However, as one British academic has noted:

> It has also been difficult to know where to draw the line between state-ments at Friday prayers that are allowed and those that are not. There is now a case of a suspect imam who the public and the police think is preaching incitement but who has been released by the High Court on very strict bail because the police have been unable to produce evidence for a specific charge.[90]

The question is "where to draw the line" *and* whether to draw the line differently when the speech is religious. While England has traditionally not imposed restrictions on free speech, does the reality of a specific threat to society require Parliament, the courts, and the police to re-consider how to effectively respond to religiously inspired terrorism?

The cases of Samina Malik and Mohammed Siddique potentially suggest that Great Britain has abandoned its historical roots of respecting free speech—particularly religious speech—in the wake of Islamic based terrorist attacks. In 2007, 23-year-old Samina Malik was convicted of "possessing records likely to be used for terrorist purposes" under the 2006 Terrorism Act. In June 2008, her conviction was overturned on appeal, and the Crown Prosecution Service decided not to seek a retrial.[91]

While in high school, Malik began writing love poems and other poetry inspired by the rap music of Americans 50 Cent and Tupac Shakur. At age 20, she became more religious and began wearing a *hijab* and calling

---

87   CNN, Bombers Target London, at http://www.cnn.com/SPECIALS/2005/london.bombing/.

88   Statement by Homeland Security Secretary Michael Chertoff announcing a change to the Nation's Threat Level for the Aviation Sector at http://www.dhs.gov/xnews/releases/pr_1158349923199.shtm.

89   *Flaming SUV rams U.K. Airport; 2 Arrests*, Associated Press, June 30, 2006.

90   Private email with author; identity known to author.

91   CPS Response to Samina Malika appeal, Crown Prosecution Service (2008-06-17), *available at* http://www.cps.gov.uk/news/pressreleases/143_08.html.

herself the "Lyrical Terrorist," later claiming that she picked the name because it "sounded cool." The documents Malik possessed included a library of books on firearms, poisons, hand-to-hand combat, and terrorism techniques. Among the documents that Malik was convicted for possessing was her poetry, in which she expressed a desire to be a martyr, an approval of beheadings, respect for Osama bin Laden, and contempt for non-Muslims. Malik has claimed that the poetry was meaningless and taken out of context, insisting that she was not a terrorist.[92] The judge termed her a "complete enigma."[93]

Mohammed Siddique was arrested on April 13, 2006 after accompanying his uncle to the Glasgow Airport. While there, the two were told they would not be allowed to fly, and Siddique's cell phone and laptop were confiscated. Siddique was charged with collecting information that would "likely be useful" to a terrorist under Section 58 (1b) of the Terrorism Act 2000. He was found guilty of "collecting terrorist-related information, setting up websites . . . and circulating inflammatory terrorist publications."

Siddique was sentenced to eight years imprisonment. His defense has consistently been that he was a merely a twenty-year-old "looking for answers," a model student who still lived with his parents. His attorneys have pointed out that there was never any evidence to support the allegation that Siddique intended to join a terrorist group. An analyst who summarized the images, documents, and videos that Siddique had downloaded said after the conviction that Siddique "lacked the skills, sophistication, lengthy credentials and cold-blooded professionalism" associated with actual terrorists, describing him as "undoubtedly naïve."[94]

The danger posed by these prosecutions is obvious. Neither Malik nor Siddique killed, much less attacked, anyone nor is there evidence that they attempted to. Yet both were convicted of serious crimes.

---

92   Lyrical Terrorist Found Guilty, BBC News, Nov. 8, 2007, *available at* http://news. bbc.co.uk/2/hi/uk_news/7084801.stm;.

93   *Id.*

94   Man convicted of terror offenses, BBC News, Sept. 17, 2007, *available at* http:// news.bbc.co.uk/2/hi/uk_news/scotland/tayside_and_central/6997830.stm; Terror Trial Hears Al-Qaeda Praise Claim, video, *available at* http://video.stv.tv/bc/ news-West_Central_Scotland-20070824-terror-trial-hears-al-qaeda-praise-claim/.

Suppose Malik and Siddique are both telling the truth—that they were simply exploring the concepts of terrorism intellectually; however, both were convicted by juries of their peers.

Great Britain is obligated to respect freedom of speech under Article 19 of the Universal Declaration of Human Rights, Article 19 of the International Covenant on Civil and Political Rights, and Article 10 of the European Convention on Human Rights. Furthermore, Great Britain has gone so far as to expressly incorporate the European Convention on Human Rights into domestic law.

Article 10 states, "Everyone has the right to freedom of expression. This right shall include freedom to hold opinions and to receive and impart information and ideas without interference by public authority and regardless of frontiers."[95] This article does, however, impose some limitations on the right:

> The exercise of these freedoms, since it carries with it duties and responsibilities, may be subject to such formalities, conditions, restrictions or penalties as are prescribed by law and are necessary in a democratic society, in the interests of national security, territorial integrity or public safety, for the prevention of disorder or crime, for the protection of health or morals, for the protection of the reputation or the rights of others, for preventing the disclosure of information received in confidence, or for maintaining the authority and impartiality of the judiciary.[96]

Going beyond the enumerated limitations of Article 10, Great Britain imposes a number of additional limitations on freedom of speech for it recognizes incitement to racial hatred and incitement to religious hatred as crimes.[97] The UK's laws on defamation are also extremely strict, imposing a high burden of proof on the defendant—one reason why many public figures who would never sue a publication in the United States regularly file suit in the United Kingdom.

95　Charter of Fundamental Rights, Article 10, *available at* http://ec.europa.eu/justice_home/unit/charte/en/charter-freedoms.html.

96　Human Rights Act, Article 8, *available at* http://news.bbc.co.uk/1/low/uk/946400.stm.

97　§§ 17–29 of the Public Order Act 1986. The Criminal Justice and Public Order Act 1994 made publication of material that incited racial hatred, a criminal offence.

Where does this leave us? As argued in this chapter, extreme religious speech presents a threat to individuals, internal communities, and society as a whole. Precisely because of the danger presented by such extremist religious speech, there is a compelling need to expand *when* religious speech may be restricted. Imposing limits, while difficult, is a must. As discussed in the chapters to come, freedom from religion warrants rearticulating the limits of individual rights in order to protect society. The best approach is to make extremist religious speech unprotected.

CHAPTER FOUR

FREEDOM OF ASSOCIATION

INTRODUCTION

The practice of public religion requires both the freedom of speech and the freedom of association. Previously, we have discussed possible limits the state can implement regarding speech. Now we turn to the freedom of association; similar to freedom of speech it must be subject to limits for the state to preserve public order in the face of religious extremism.

Religious worship can be divided into two categories—individual and group. Individual worship includes personal prayer, fasting, and charitable giving. Group worship includes church attendance and prayer groups. This chapter addresses whether limits should be imposed on the freedom of group association in the name of religion.

Freedom of association is guaranteed by the U.S. Constitution; in addition, the Supreme Court has expressly held that "the freedom to engage in association for the advancement of beliefs and ideas is an inseparable aspect of the 'liberty' assured by the Due Process Clause of the Fourteenth Amendment, which embraces freedom of speech."[1] Liberal democracy is premised on the right of individuals to gather, assemble, and associate with when, where, and with whom they desire.[2] This principle is similarly guaranteed by international treaties including the International Covenant on Civil and Political Rights.[3]

When limits are imposed on the right of people to gather for express purposes, such limits are premised on considerations that require balancing the rights of the individual with the obligation of the state to protect

---

1   *NAACP v. Alabama ex rel. Patterson*, 357 U.S. 449 (1958).

2   "Congress shall make no law respecting an establishment of religion, or prohibiting the free exercise thereof; or abridging the freedom of speech, or of the press; or the right of the people peaceably to assemble, and to petition the Government for a redress of grievances" First Amendment, U.S. Constitution.

3   ICCPR, Arts. 21, 22.

other citizens.[4] When fundamental rights are affected, the state must demonstrate a compelling interest to so limit; implementation must be narrowly tailored to achieve that state interest. In the event where the state's primary interest is to protect the rights of other citizens, the court will generally uphold the law.[5] This level of judicial review is the strict scrutiny discussed earlier.

For liberal democracies, the suggestion that limits can be imposed on speech in a house of worship is highly problematic. Limiting the right of people of faith to assemble at their preferred house of worship would be an extraordinary additional restriction on how religion is practiced. However, if places of worship are centers of religious-based incitement, the state must be ready to limit access as a legitimate means to protect society. Therefore, as I argued earlier in the case of free speech, Intermediate Scrutiny, instead of Strict Scrutiny, should apply to the freedom of *association* as well.

THE DANGERS OF ASSEMBLY

Faith, as defined and articulated by religious leaders in sermons, study groups, or other religious activities, can justify and incite violence against individuals and groups. This violence can be directed toward those outside the religious community, as in the case of Paul Hill, the pastor convicted of murdering a physician performing abortions. The violence can also be directed toward members of an internal community, as in the case of the FLDS Church, where underage girls are married to adult men. The danger specifically associated with assembly is that words of incitement take place within a closed community, beyond the sight of a watchful police force, courts, or legislature.

While some people of faith gather for weekly religious study groups in private homes, the most common meeting place for prayer is in a church, synagogue, or mosque. What are churches, synagogues, and mosques? They are public places of worship where people of faith come to express

---

4   *See Larson v. Valente*, 456 U.S. 228, 102 S. Ct. 1673, 72 L. Ed. 2d 33 (1982); *Wisconsin v. Yoder*, 406 U.S. 205, 92 S. Ct. 1526, 32 L. Ed. 2d 15 (1972); *Sherbert v. Verner*, 374 U.S. 398, 83 S. Ct. 1790, 10 L. Ed. 2d 965, 9 Fair Empl. Prac. Cas. (BNA) 1152 (1963) and (limited on other grounds by, *Employment Div., Dept. of Human Resources of Oregon v. Smith*, 494 U.S. 872, 110 S. Ct. 1595 (1990)).

5   *Cantwell v. State of Connecticut*, 310 U.S. 296 (1940).

and share their belief with fellow congregants, to manifest their sense of cultural-religious identity, to pray and reflect; it is a house of worship.[6] But these buildings—churches, synagogues, and mosques—are more than just places of worship. They are public gathering places for social events as well. Places of worship serve as food kitchens, meeting places for Alcoholics Anonymous and Boy Scouts. In these host capacities, they serve the public good. It must be acknowledged, however, that they have also been centers for espousing violence, as is the case with religious extremism.

Communal prayer is one of the fundamental tenets of public religious life and represents a critical venue for how individuals collectively express and practice their religion. Places of worship are where people of faith gather and practice their religion. Squaring the right to peaceful assembly with the knowledge that some of assemblies are not peaceful is the fundamental dilemma when recommending limiting that right, particularly in the context of religious assembly.

WHEN CAN THE STATE LIMIT ASSEMBLY?

When public religion and assembly are used to incite or propel others to violence, that speech—even if religion based—must be limited. The designated leader of a religious community—whether priest, pastor, rabbi, or imam—has extraordinary influence over his or her congregation. Precisely because of this critical role, the actions and speech of the clergy warrant special attention even to the extent of limiting the freedom and right to assemble and associate. Most sermons are interpretations of sacred texts seeking to discern God's guidance and direction. These sermons, at their most inspiring, are faith based, seeking to move the listener to a fuller experience of God, life, and other people. However, when the religious leader preaches, directly or indirectly, violence against specific people or groups, then the leader is inciting violent behavior which must be prevented.

---

6   The right to erect and use a modern church building may in a proper case include a parking lot for the use of members in attending church services and any meetings held by the church, and all such rooms and facilities under one roof as ordinarily form and constitute a part of the building or equipment and are deemed necessary or useful in connection with a modern church of the particular denomination involved. *Keeling v. Board of Zoning Appeals* (1946) 117 IND APP 314, 69 NE2d 613.

When does religious belief become dangerous? This question cannot be considered in a vacuum, for the systematic limitation of religious belief requires curtailing how, when, and where religion is practiced. J.P. Larsen has written:

> One of the most central tenets of religion is its unconditional belief in truth, which is also one of the most fundamental violence-conducive elements of religion. To understand the underlying reason for this, it is important to remember that religions do not merely 'claim' to profess truth, as most secular observers argue; rather, it is for them an undeniable reality. . . . For a religion, its truth is not only more valid than the claims of other systems of thought, but it must necessarily be the *only* valid belief.[7]

If the state limits the practice of extreme religious belief, and association in the name of that belief, is it not limiting what an individual can believe? And if so, is that not an inexcusable violation of political, civil, and human rights? What religious belief system can justify such a brutal attack by the state on the essence of the human condition?

> It is universal of all religions to lay claim to truth. Where the monotheistic religions (the focus of this book) may be more extreme (and thus violent) in relation to their truth is that such truth does not recognize the validity of any other truth.[8]

Does that mean that the test for determining when and how the state can limit the practice of religious belief is limited only to when people of faith become violent? If there is a direct relationship between religious faith, truth, and violence, then in order to ensure public order and personal security, the point of intervention should take place *before* violence occurs.

While "anonymous worshippers"[9] do not inherently endanger society, people of faith who subscribe to religious extremism do. In *Yosifof v. Attorney General*, Justice Landau of the Israel Supreme Court wrote, "the freedom of conscience and worship is one of the individual's liberties

---

7   J.P. Larsen, Understanding Religious Violence—Thinking Outside the Box on Terrorism, Ashgate, 2004; 110.

8   Larsen, 111.

9   Scott Atran, *In Gods We Trust* (Oxford University Press, 2002), 151.

assured in every enlightened democratic regime."[10] Similarly, U.S. Chief Justice Stone in *United States v. MacIntosh* wrote:

> All our history gives confirmation to the view that liberty of conscience has a moral and social value which makes it worthy of preservation at the hands of the state. So deep in its significance and vital indeed is it to the integrity of men's moral and spiritual nature that nothing short of the self-preservation of the state should warrant its violation.[11]

A house of worship does not grant faith leaders immunity; a synagogue is not a sanctuary for hate-speech, a mosque is not a haven for *fatwas*, and a church is not a stage for a pastor to encourage congregants to commit crimes in the name of religion. However, precisely because all three examples are not abstract but rather concrete manifestations of *where and how* faith is practiced, places of worship are not immune from examination. If faith leaders are inciting congregants to acts of violence against both general and specific targets then it is no longer protected religious speech as the incitement to violence justifies the state's decision to limit it.

Throughout history the church, synagogue, and mosque have been places of learning, peaceful gathering, and creative non-violence. Certainly the preaching and leadership of the Rev. Martin Luther King Jr. is a testament to religious faith at its best. Yet we do not have to go back centuries to find examples of religious violence. For every Martin Luther King Jr., there is a Pope Urban II, who declared that it was God's will to kill the infidel and reclaim Jerusalem for Christendom. Those "who got in the way" of the crusader—Jew, Muslim or Christian heretic—were defined as "infidel." In Europe, anti-Semitism was on the lips of untold ministers for years. David Kertzer has argued that the Catholic Church adhered to a distinction between "good anti-Semitism" and "bad anti-Semitism."[12] Opinions are legitimate, disagreement is healthy but when assembly endangers others, the state must limit that otherwise guaranteed right.

---

10   As cited in Religion in the Public Sphere: A Comparative Analysis of German, Israeli, American and International Law, *The Model of State and Church Relations and Its Impact on the Protection of Freedom of Conscience and Religion: A Comparative Analysis and a Case Study of Israel*, Shimon Shetreet (Springer, 2007), 124.

11   *Id.* at 115.

12   David Kertzer, *The Popes Against the Jews: The Vatican's Role in the Rise of Modern Anti-Semitism* (Random House, 2001).

Even if the assembly is occurring in a house of worship; particularly when the basis is religious extremism.

BALANCING RIGHTS AND THE STATE'S OBLIGATIONS

When religious words or actions threaten the safety of individuals, the state has an overwhelming duty to step in. In balancing between the right to religious practice and the right to be free from extreme religious belief, the issue is one of line-drawing. Martha Minow writes:

> Yet tolerance seems so much better than it's opposite. Intolerance, the dictionary tells us, entails the "unwillingness or refusal to tolerate or respect contrary opinions or beliefs, persons of different races or backgrounds." To be intolerant is to be bigoted, which, in one of those unhelpfully circular dictionary definitions, means being "so obstinately attached to a creed, opinion or practice as to be illiberal or intolerant." Intolerance is scolding and degrading; it plants seeds for harassment and even violence. In this difficult first decade of a new century, intolerance of immigrants, headscarves, and political dissenters is palpable in politics, in the media, and even in classrooms. Abortion clinics are sites of intolerance and, at times, violent protest; right-to-life protesters can also name their own ample encounters with intolerance. Growing rights for gays, lesbians, and other sexual minorities meet with overt expressions of hatred and intolerance.

> Some theorists place tolerance as the precondition for equality, freedom and justice. Then intolerance deserves the most serious response. But we soon hit the dilemma: the most serious response to intolerance is to stop it, to refuse to endure it, to object, scorn, to become intolerant. Tolerance was supposed to endure the objectionable and establish peaceful co-existence with disagreeable others. How can the tolerant be intolerant of intolerance? But how can the tolerant tolerate intolerance?[13]

The question is, ultimately, one of balancing. What endangers society-limiting freedoms of a particular group (religious extremists) or protecting the larger public? In the tolerance/intolerance debate—in the context of the danger posed by religious extremism to the larger community—perhaps we should "err on the side of caution." In that sense, the appropriate response to Prof. Minow is greater intolerance with respect to intolerance. However, that approach immediately raises deep—and highly justified—concerns regarding the true face of liberal democracies.

---

13   Martha Minow, *Tolerance in an Age of Terror*, 16 S. Cal. Interdisc. L.J. 453, 458–59 (Spring 2007).

How do democracies resolve the fundamental tension between free exercise and the establishment clause and what is the price of its resolution to freedom?

TURKEY

In Turkey, religious fundamentalism is seen as a direct threat to the secular state. Turkey has taken firm action to control religious leaders. Imams are required "to complete formal studies where the secular government establishes the curriculum, and are *only* allowed to preach if they have a government-provided license."[14] The salaries of the imams are paid by the government as "another instrument of control."[15]

Just as the Turkish Constitution defines and resolves the tension between the fundamental right of religion and the secular state in favor of the secular state[16] the Constitution also enumerates the state's right to curtail the freedom of association. Under the Turkish Constitution, free association may only be curtailed "on the grounds of protecting national security and public order, or prevention of crime commitment, or protecting public morals, public health."[17] In the context of association in the name of religion, Turkey has actively limited assembly/association under the color of the law. For example, in 2000 a "Christian congregation in Gaziantep . . . encountered difficulty in obtaining permission to hold services. One member of the group was briefly detained for allegedly bribing people to convert to Christianity."[18] Also in 2000, several Christians in Istanbul continue to stand trial on the charge of "illegal assembly" for holding church and bible study meetings in an apartment."[19]

---

14   Michael Radu, *Radical Imams and Terrorists*, FOREIGN POLICY RESEARCH INSTITUTE, Watch on the West, Vol 6, No. 6, August 2005, *available at* http://www.fpri.org/ww/0606.200508.radu.imamsterrorists.html, last visited October 5, 2008.

15   *Id.*

16   *See* CONSTITUTION OF TURKEY, Article 14, Prohibition of Abuse of Fundamental Rights and Freedoms.

17   CONSTITUTION OF TURKEY, Article 33, Freedom of Association.

18   *Turkey: International Religious Freedom Report, 2001*, Bureau of Democracy, Human Rights and Labor, Department of the State, October 26, 2001, *available at* http://www.state.gov/g/drl/rls/irf/2001/5694.htm, last visited October 6, 2008.

19   *Id.*

In addition, some religious minority groups have a difficult time holding services. Turkish codes mandate that "only the Government can designate a place of worship, and if a religion has no legal standing in the country, it may not be eligible for a designated site."[20] Non-Muslim religious services, especially for religious groups that do not own property recognized by the [government] often take place on diplomatic property or in private apartments. Police occasionally barred Christians from holding services in private apartments, and prosecutors have opened cases against Christians for holding unauthorized gatherings."[21] Further, the Turkish government has actively banned membership in certain religious groups. For example, "Mystical Sufi and other religious-social orders (tarikats) and lodges (cemaats) have been banned officially since the mid-1920s."[22]

Recently, Turkey took steps to curtail political association believed to be in the name of religion and thus a threat to the secular state.[23] "In March 2008 the chief prosecutor filed a case against the ruling AKP (Justice and Development Party) to close the party, claiming that it has become a 'center of 'antisecular' activities.' According to Article 68 of the Constitution, 'the activities of political parties shall not be in conflict with . . . the principles of the democratic and secular republic.' While the prosecutor acknowledged that the AKP's program and its written statutes were not unconstitutional, the indictment charged that AKP had 'in actions and verbal statements acted against laws and the Constitution.'"[24]

---

20   *Turkey: International Religious Freedom Report, 2008*, Bureau of Democracy, Human Rights and Labor, Department of the State, September 19, 2008, *available at* http://www.state.gov/g/drl/rls/irf/2008/108476.htm, last visited October 6, 2008.

21   *Id.*

22   *Turkey: International Religious Freedom Report, 2008*, Bureau of Democracy, Human Rights and Labor, Department of the State, September 19, 2008, *available at* http://www.state.gov/g/drl/rls/irf/2008/108476.htm, last visited October 6, 2008.

23   For more information on the history of secularism in Turkey, see the Appendix.

24   *Turkey: International Religious Freedom Report, 2008*, Bureau of Democracy, Human Rights and Labor, Department of the State, September 19, 2008, *available at* http://www.state.gov/g/drl/rls/irf/2008/108476.htm, last visited October 6, 2008.

Ultimately, the ruling AKP party was kept alive by one vote on the Constitutional Court. However, "the court reined the party in, imposing a strong but not fatal sanction to cut its public financing in half and issuing a 'serious warning' that it was steering the country in too Islamic a direction. Legislation pressed by the party that would have allowed women in head scarves to attend universities, for example, raised suspicions about its agenda."[25]

As previously discussed, Turkey's geo-political significance is extraordinary. Therefore, the secular-religious tension in Turkey is of enormous importance both to Turks and the international community. In an effort to minimize increasing religious extremism the Turkish state is limiting freedom of association believed to advance religiosity in Turkey. Not only is religious speech of concern to the secular state, but religious based association is similarly perceived to be a threat.

THE UNITED STATES

Only in extreme cases will the U.S. limit or restrict the right of citizens to meet in the advancement of a mutual goal or idea. Courts examine limitations on free association using a strict scrutiny standard.[26] Freedom of association is most deeply impacted when the government attempts to outlaw particular groups and punish individuals for joining those groups. The Supreme Court held that the government may only punish group membership if it proves that the individual in question is actively affiliated with Group X, that the individual knows of Group X's illegal objectives, and the individual possesses specific intent to further Group X's objectives.[27] Returning to the speech analysis from the previous chapter, the Supreme Court has held that where Group X's activities fall

---

25   Sabrina Tavernise, *Turkish Court Calls Ruling Party Constitutional*, New York Times, July 31, 2008.

26   As mentioned previously, strict scrutiny demands that the government show (1) a sufficiently important, or compelling governmental interest, *Timmons v. Twin Cities Area New Party*, 520 U.S. 351 (1997); (2) that the means used are narrowly tailored to accomplish the governmental interest, *Buckley v. Valeo*, 424 U.S. 1 (1976); and (3) there is no less restrictive means to satisfy the compelling governmental interest *State ex rel. Billings v. City of Point Pleasant*, 194 W. Va. 301, 460 S.E.2d 436 (1995).

27   Erwin Chemerinsky, Constitutional Law, 1396, citing *Scales v. United States*, 367 U.S. 203 (1961).

short of illegal incitement, and consist merely of advocacy of abstract ideas, group membership cannot be punished.[28]

Furthermore, under the current test, an individual has a constitutionally protected right to be part of any political or religious group, even if it embraces illegal and violent goals, provided that the individual does not plan to act in furtherance of illegal purposes.[29] While this test empowers the government to prevent incitement, the "line in the sand" is drawn very closely to the edge of a precarious cliff, leaving little room between violent speech and violent action.[30]

Similarly, the Supreme Court also addressed the question of whether the government can require disclosure of group membership. In *NAACP v. State of Alabama ex rel. Patterson*,[31] the Court held that disclosure can only be forced when the government meets the aforementioned strict scrutiny standard. The Court noted the "close nexus between the freedoms of speech and assembly," and that "it is hardly a novel perception that compelled disclosure of affiliation with groups engaged in advocacy may constitute as effective a restraint on freedom of association." However, the Court did note in *NAACP* that the organization did not object to "divulging the identity of its members who are employed by or hold official positions with it. [The NAACP] has urged the rights solely of its ordinary rank-and-file members."[32]

Under *NAACP*, could the government demand the names of clergy members of a religious extremist group? Initially, it would seem that that the answer is "maybe." Abiding by a strict scrutiny standard, the burden would be on the government to show that it had a compelling interest in protecting either members of the religious communities or outsiders from violence.

Public religion is predicated on people of the same faith congregating at their desired house of worship for communal prayer. The constitution and case law upholds this right. However, religious extremists assembled in a house of worship have profoundly impacted the freedom

---

28   Erwin Chemerinsky, Constitutional Law, 1397, citing *Noto v. United States*, 367 U.S. 290 (1961).

29   *Green v. Connally*, 404 U.S. 997 (1971).

30   For additional discussion of Freedom of Assembly, see the Appendix.

31   357 U.S. 449 (1958)

32   For a more in-depth discussion of *NAACP v. Alabama*, see the Appendix.

of association. By inciting violence, religious extremists will increasingly force the government to limit the right of religious association. To that end, the strict scrutiny standard may provide religious extremists unwarranted and unjustified "immunity" with respect to freedom of assembly. The freedom of assembly facilitates a dangerous confluence between religious extremism and houses of worship. Precisely for that reason, freedom from religion suggests that freedom of assembly be limited when that right is abused in the furtherance of extremism and violence.

CHAPTER FIVE

THE ROLE OF THE MEDIA REGARDING RELIGION

INTRODUCTION

Today more than ever, the media can affect the opinions of innumerable portions of the population. The manner in which the media covers religion and its effects on society can directly lead to shifts in the general public's attitude of extremist ideas and actions. This chapter examines how the media portrays religion, religious extremists, and religious violence.

Traditionally, religion has been out of bounds,[1] not openly and candidly discussed in public. This code of silence on religious issue, while "polite," does not serve society well. Because of the inherent tension and controversy surrounding religion, having an intelligent, informed discussion regarding religion requires laying aside many stereotypes, false assumptions, and illusions. This discussion must be based on facts and accuracy. This is, in part, where the press comes in.

There is no systematic journalistic monitoring of extremist religious terrorist *threats*, only coverage *after* a major event occurs. As the 9/11 Commission Report pointed out, "all this reportage looked backward, describing problems satisfactorily resolved." Coverage of potential attacks increased toward the end of 1999, but as the millennium passed without

---

1   Private email, date and content in my records, "The 'traditional' media of newspapers and local/network TV have relied too much over the years on the same 'official spokespeople' when reporting on issues such as religion and race. This is less true now than it used to be, but for a long time—as an example—certain individuals were trotted out as the official spokesman for African-Americans. That one person could provide a 'black' viewpoint was preposterous. The same has been true in covering religion. All the major faiths are highly fragmented and it is silly to think that any one person can provide a Jewish, Catholic, or Muslim point of view. There are millions of Evangelical Christians who are not represented by Pat Robertson, Jerry Falwell, or the other televangelists. This type of coverage is driven in part by the small amount of space and time that newspapers and local/network TV devote to any one story and the factors that you discuss in that religion is a topic that people do not want to discuss or read about."

incident, the stories ebbed. Even following the bombing of the USS Cole, coverage of the overall threat of religious terrorism posed to the United States dwindled.[2]

Has the media tended to ignore the dangers posed by religious extremists? In some cases yes, in other cases no. Two examples regarding this question are illuminating. First, prior to the assassination of Yitzhak Rabin, the Israeli press gave the extreme religious right a relative "pass" regarding their advocacy of violence as it failed to warn of the dangers posed by religious extremists. Second, in contrast to the Israeli press coverage of extreme rabbis, the American press has been relatively diligent in covering the FLDS church and the dangers posed, particularly to church members.

WHAT IS THE MEDIA?

When discussing the media in the context of extreme religion, it is important to define the separate and distinct sources of media outlets. Today, the word "media" encompasses extraordinarily diverse information sources. As suggested by one student of the media:

> The "media" is so fragmented and diverse that it doesn't make sense to talk about them as some unified group. The space/time that a particular news medium can devote to a story and the audience that it is directed to varies widely. A daily newspaper or local/network daily news show has limited space and time to cover stories and is trying to be "everything to everybody". Gannett papers like *USA Today* and *The Arizona Republic* rarely run stories that are over 12 inches long. A 20-inch story is considered a long one. Obviously, this format does not lend itself to reporting on complicated and nuanced issues. Magazines (*The Atlantic, New Yorker*), websites, cable TV (Discovery Channel, CNN), and NPR are better able to report on issues involving religion, but their audience(s) are far smaller and are niches of particular demographics. CNN has done some excellent documentaries about religion.[3]

The forms of media have progressively changed over the last century. News sources were comprised solely of major newspapers and weekly news magazines; radio and television soon followed. Specialized media focused on specific audiences, representing particular philosophical

---

2   AMOS N. GUIORA, FUNDAMENTALS OF COUNTERTERRORISM (2008).

3   Private email sent to author; date and content in author's records.

or ideological beliefs. In the last 25 years, with the introduction of cable television and the Internet, the term "media" has significantly expanded.[4]

---

4   Daniel C. Barr, Perkins Coie Brown & Bain, email correspondence with the author, July 21, 2008; email in my records. Barr further suggested:

> I wouldn't characterize the difference as that between newspapers and websites. The websites of the *New York Times, Wall Street Journal*, etc., have the same standards as their print versions. Assuming we are talking about the differences between newspapers and blogs/websites run by a small handful of people, or even one person, the big difference in my mind is the role that collective judgment plays and at what stage that collective judgment occurs. With the traditional media (papers, TV, and their respective websites), the collective judgment occurs BEFORE the story is published or aired. The story is discussed internally beforehand between the reporter and editors and between the editors themselves. Once written, the story is reviewed and edited by several editors and perhaps by a lawyer like me. With the new media, the collective judgment occurs AFTER the story is published. Someone posts something on a blog and other blogs started adding, detracting, or knocking down the story. The editing process occurs in and among the public and among people who may or may not be knowledgeable about what they are talking about. Put in another context, think of the difference between the Encyclopedia Britannica and Wikipedia. The editing of the former occurs before publication. The editing of the latter occurs after publication and is constantly ongoing.
>
> To illustrate what I am talking about, how the blogosphere "edits" stories, take a look at the blog my son Andrew writes for "The Briefing Room," http://briefingroom.thehill.com/. The Briefing Room is an effort by *The Hill* to do a blog about what is being said during the day about political stories on other political blogs. It is a blog about other blogs. One some days, you can see how certain stories morph throughout the day.
>
> One of the big items that is being "edited" rather poorly by the blogoshpere are the claims that Obama is a Muslim. Such a claim would not initially get published in the traditional media because the internal editing process would determine it to be false. In the new media, however, the rumor that Obama is a Muslim gets reported as fact, is spread to other websites and blogs and shared with who knows how many people by email. Despite the efforts of others in the traditional and new media to "edit" this story, to prove that it is false, there is still a significant minority of people out there who believe that Obama is a Muslim.
>
> One of the other big differences between the traditional and "new" media is that the traditional media makes much more of an effort to separate opinion from fact. People may disagree about how successful some papers and TV news outlets do that, but at least they try. However, many blogs and websites intertwine objective fact with opinion. They are effectively op-ed pages. This type of advocacy journalism has made its way onto cable TV news, such as Fox News or "Countdown," the Keith Olberman show on MSNBC".

In the American setting, the new Huntley-Brinkley,[5] Edward Murrow, and Walter Cronkite[6] that ruled the air waves and set the tone for news reporting in the 1960s and '70s, are CNN, FOX-News, the Internet, and bloggers. They have become the primary news sources for millions of Americans and audiences worldwide. Cable news programs work on a 24-hour cycle, which has led to criticism for under-reporting of serious issues as news is increasingly delivered in an entertainment-based format.

Today's non-traditional media, unlike traditional outlets, which are subject to regulations, is unregulated; this is particularly relevant to the blogosphere as bloggers seek to shock the audience. Given the reach and style of bloggers their ability to affect public opinion is dramatically different than mainstream, media outlets. Their impact ability is heightened both because of the immediacy of their reporting and its inherently unfiltered nature.[7]

The Internet has proven particularly successful in ensuring unlimited distribution of pictures that the mainstream media would not air. Daniel Pearl's[8] beheading is a classic and tragic example. While the overwhelming majority of Internet sites refused to post the beheading, a small number did.[9] Since Daniel Pearl, the Internet has continued to provide video of the beheadings of other Western targets—examples include Nicholas Berg, Kenneth Bigley, Jack Hensley, and Eugene Armstrong. Why? Obviously some sites seek to satisfy morbid curiosity, and while

---

5   NBC News Nightly News, 1956–1970.

6   CBS News, 1962–1981.

7   While the same rules apply to websites, Section 230 of the Communications Decency Act gives immunity to a website for publishing third party content on a message board or as comments as long as the operators of the website do not edit the third party content. The people who post the third party on the message board, however, are subject to the same libel and privacy laws as everyone else.

8   *Available at* http://www.meforum.org/article/713, last visited July 21, 2008.

9   According to one commentator (private email, date and content in author's records), "there are no decency standards on the web or in print. In the U.S., the FCC imposes decency standards on broadcasters, but not on cable. That's why people can swear on HBO. CNN.com or HBO or the *New York Times* could have carried photos of Pearl's beheading if they had wanted to. In fact, the *Dallas Morning News* DID carry a photo of one of the earlier beheadings in Iraq with the guy holding the severed head aloft. The *Dallas Morning News* had every legal right to do so. Not surprisingly, however, many readers were upset with them for doing so."

this is troubling, it is not the primary problem issue as larger, more significant interests are at stake. Simply stated, from the perspective of al Qaeda and its supporters, few images are more effective, convincing, and powerful than the beheading of Daniel Pearl, whose last recorded words were "I am a Jew."[10]

Secondary sources aired this video for a variety of reasons. Perhaps they intended to facilitate the initial terrorist group goals of recruiting new members, showing the organization's vitality to existing membership and warning the U.S. (and allies) of the organization's power and determination. While the websites that posted this are not considered traditional media, they are the contemporary means by which news is transmitted. Websites that posted the beheading are important propaganda tools, perhaps similar to Soviet-era newspapers, informing and therefore shaping the public debate. Because websites, whether they engage in self-imposed restraints or not, are sources of information to the public their importance cannot be minimized.[11]

HOW DOES THE MEDIA TREAT RELIGION?

In the main, when the media reports an event with religious undertones, coverage falls into one of five categories: (1) hysteria, (2) political correctness, (3) dismissiveness, (4) deference, and (5) in-depth, balanced reporting. When a media outlet engages in hysteria, it fans the flames of an already tense situation. Political correctness similarly can be dangerous, as the media declines to delve deeply into an issue for fear of offending subjects and viewers alike due to the sensitive nature of many religious issues. Dismissiveness is also common for many members of the media are secular and find it difficult to connect with religious cultures.[12] Conversely, the media can be overly deferential to the particular religion in question and are therefore fearful of describing it in a potentially negative light. Obviously, the fifth option, objective reporting, is the ideal.

It is necessary to examine why the media engages in the first four categories to understand the role it plays with respect to religious extremism. Otherwise, it will be very difficult to determine why the media is either

---

10   AMOS N. GUIORA, FUNDAMENTALS OF COUNTERTERRORISM (2009).

11   AMOS N. GUIORA, FUNDAMENTALS OF COUNTERTERRORISM, (2009).

12   Suggested by a member of the media in a private email correspondence with the author, date and contents in author's records.

willing or hesitant to criticize religious groups. Are certain topics "off-limits" for fear of being accused of anti-Semitism, bigotry or fear-mongering? Perhaps this explains why some media outlets exhibit hesitation to criticize many of the negative events that have arisen in the context of religion. Such failure raises concern that the media fails to report known information in order to avoid controversy, conflict, or irritate powerful constituencies.

One member of the media suggested the following:

> When talking about the objectives/goals/purposes of the media, both among newer forms as well as "traditional" forms, media organizations have varying objectives. Some are trying to make money (most are). Others are non-profits, by definition of their mission-statement at least. Some seek to inform, other to educate (slightly different). Some seek to entertain. A whole new genre of "infotainment" has arisen in the past twenty years, and has reached new heights with the Internet.[13]

For example if a media outlet engages in hysteria, portraying "Islam as a threat" without distinguishing between mainstream and extremism beliefs, or between Sunn'i and Shi'a, then the public is ill-served. While perhaps this sort of sensationalism is an effective means to sell newspapers, it does not contribute to rational public debate. "Political correctness" is equally unhelpful, for it distorts issues and denies the legitimacy of criticism. Those who placate extremists are as unhelpful as those who engage in hysteria. It is critical that the media differentiate between mainstream religion and religious extremism.

It has been argued that such impartial and impassionate coverage is not always appropriate. For example, Ida B. Wells reported on the lynching of African-American men in the late 19th and early 20th centuries. She argued that regarding some issues; such as lynching, it was not necessary to explore the alternative viewpoint. It is important to note that "dispassionate reflection" is not the only perspective the media can or should take. The media can take an "observer" position (reflected by current attitudes of the mainstream media), a commentator position (reflected by Wells' attitude), or any number of positions falling in between. Which approach is critical as that will best serve society's interests, it must also be one that journalists should find most meaningful

---

13   Private email sent to author; date and content in author's records.

and worthwhile. Of the models outlined in the table below, I recommend Mill's:

Observer <=> Commentator

Rawlsian:	Aristotelian:	Kantian:	John Stuart Mill:	Ida B. Wells:
John Rawls proposed the idea of the "veil of ignorance." This view holds that the journalist must imagine which rules they would want followed if they weren't journalists. Also described as "justice as fairness."	Espouses moderation, neither overtly deferential nor dismissive toward religious subjects of media coverage.	Asks, "To whom does the journalist owe a duty?" Also, two categorical imperatives must be kept in mind: (1) The journalist should act as if his/her action would lead to a universal law to which all others would adhere; (2) Individuals should always be treated as an end and never as a means.	Suggests journalists should seek the greatest contribution to the general welfare.	Wrote that some stories involved inherently evil subject matter— lynching of African-Americans in Wells' time— and therefore it was not necessary to seek out that side of the story.

THE ISRAELI PRESS

The Israeli media has historically treated Jewish religious extremists gingerly. In the aftermath of Rabin's murder, there was a sense amongst Israeli journalists of "Where were we?" Did Israeli journalists sufficiently report the unending and unyielding incitement against Rabin engineered by the extreme religious right? Did journalists take these extremist groups seriously, or did they shrug them off and dismiss them as the ranting of a lunatic fringe incapable of action? By failing to take the threat seriously, the Israeli media gave the extreme right a free pass. According to one senior Israeli journalist[14] the Israeli media's efforts to scrutinize and criticize rabbis who granted Yigal Amir legitimacy and

---

14   Private conversation, date and source in author's records.

guidance is best described as "gentle."[15] The reason, according to the journalist, is a direct mirroring of the unwillingness by the State Attorney's office to file indictments for incitement: journalists did not want to provoke the religious right.

As one thoughtful observer of the Israeli media suggested:

> Something to keep in mind regarding the sometime[s] dismissive attitude of the media toward the religious zealots: most reporters are secular liberals. They find it difficult to "connect" with the culture of the religious camp and are sometimes tempted to dismiss them as a bunch of lunatics, thus not taking seriously the ability of these "lunatics" to take actions that change the course of history.[16]

The rise of messianic right-wing politics gave birth in the mid-1970s to the extreme movement Gush Emunim, which in turn led to the Jewish terrorist underground of the 1980s. When the underground was uncovered by the General Security Services (GSS, today referred to as Israel Security Agency) in April 1984, its members had already carried out attacks on Palestinians, including several Arab mayors in the West Bank and was planning to destroy the Dome of the Rock mosque in Jerusalem.[17] Not only were innocent Palestinians the targets of the groups' attacks, but on at least one occasion an Israeli Border Policeman[18] was injured when group members deliberately did not warn him of a bomb they had placed in a car he was checking.

While the Israeli media was experienced in reporting on Palestinian (internal and external alike) terrorism, a Jewish extremist religious-based terrorist organization presented important and substantially different challenges. From the media perspective, the traditional paradigm had been turned upside down—rather than Palestinians attacking innocent Israelis, Israelis were attacking innocent Palestinians.

What made the religious extremist organization extraordinarily dangerous was that its fringe elements were involved in planning an attack whose consequences could literally engulf the Middle East in a war. The group's

---

15   Private conversation, date and source in author's records.

16   Private email; date and source in author's records.

17   Jeffrey Heller, Israel PM sees threat from "Jewish underground", NewsDaily at http://www.newsdaily.com/stories/tre48r1cd-us-israel-olmert-underground/.

18   Border Police are part of the national police force.

operational plan to blow up the Dome of the Rock[19] is the manifestation of religious extremist terrorism. The media however did not attack the rabbis who provided the ideological, religious justification for the attacks. The media did not subject those whose teachings served as the basis for attacks on innocent civilians—based on interpretation of religious text—to extensive scrutiny and criticism.

The importance of this cannot—nor should not—be minimized. As this book's thesis suggests, religious extremism is fundamentally and existentially different from secular terrorism for it lays claim to acting in the name of the divine. For that very reason the media—traditional and non-traditional alike—have a responsibility to report and comment on religious extremist terrorism fundamentally differently than its coverage to date. Unquestionably, 9/11 was a terrible attack. However, it did not threaten societies to the extent that blowing up the Dome of the Rock would. The conflagration that would result from such an attack is literally unparalleled and would—within minutes—spiral out of control with no foreseeable mitigation.

What was the Israeli media doing in the face of this possible attack? The answer, according to *both* members of the media and students of the press is uniformly unanimous: *nothing*. The failure to fully address the threat in all of its unimaginable parameters is the "poster child" for media unwillingness or perhaps inability to fully comprehend the extraordinary danger that religious extremism presents.

When applying this example to the five categories above, it clearly fits the "dismissing" of threat and actors alike. The media's colloquial self-explanation as to why the story did not merit their fullest attention would be "these 'nut jobs' can't be serious." According to another senior Israeli journalist, the reasons for this failure are two-fold: the media largely took its cues from the State Attorney's office, and secondly, the belief that blowing up the Dome of the Rock would be an "unimaginable" act of terrorism. Regardless of the reasons, the media failed to accurately and fully report on an operational plan of unimaginable proportions and dangers.[20] Simply put, the mainstream Israeli media gave the rabbis a "pass" with respect to their support of the Jewish Underground.

---

19   Inside the Dome of the Rock (Masjid Qubbat As-Sakhrah) is the rock from which the prophet Muhammed is believed to have ridden on his horse to heaven; it is one of Islam's three holiest sites.

20   Private conversation, content and date in author's records.

AMERICAN MEDIA COVERAGE OF THE FLDS CHURCH

The Fundamentalist Church of Jesus Christ of Latter-Day Saints (FLDS) as well as the religion from which it stems has had a long and sometimes difficult history with media coverage.

In April 2008, government authorities received an anonymous call from an underage girl claiming that she had been forced to marry into a polygamous relationship with a much older man. This call led to a raid on the FLDS compound, Yearning for Zion, in Eldorado, Texas. In the immediate aftermath of the raid, the media's extensive coverage was primarily focused on the issue of sexual relations between adult male members of the Church and what was presumed to be underage girls. This was similar to the media's coverage of the Warren Jeffs' trial for accomplice to rape stemming from a marriage he conducted between Elissa Wall, then 14, and Allen Steed, her 19-year-old cousin.

Though there was extensive media coverage condemning the actions of FLDS members, the essence of the coverage was the criminal activity of a number of individuals. While the seriousness of those allegations should not be minimized, they are not the core issue. The primary issue *not* covered by the media was criminal activity in the name of religious extremism. Simply put, the sensationalism that FLDS members regularly had sex with underage girls was perceived as more compelling than the religious extremism commanding that underage girls be regularly violated. In other words, coverage of underage sex and its inherent sensationalism won out over coverage of the underlying danger posed by religious extremism and its effect on the entire community and, in particular, otherwise unprotected and vulnerable underage girls.

Why? To answer that question in the context of the five categories of media coverage, it is necessary to examine the relationship between the FLDS Church and mainstream American media. Doing so raises uncomfortable questions regarding assumptions, presumptions, and stereotypes. Quite frankly it is a tale of how the media covers the "others" whose beliefs and practices have historically been perceived as a challenge to traditional Christianity.

Because of that perceived challenge, the media, much like mainstream American culture and society, has had a skeptical (if not hostile) perception of the FLDS Church as well as the Church of Jesus Christ of Latter-Day Saints (the Mormon Church). The largely (if not overwhelmingly) negative attitude regarding the Church is predicated on a number of issues that individually and collectively have significantly affected how the Church has been perceived and portrayed by the media.[21]

The sources of skepticism, if not disdain, from the perspective of "mainstream" America are easily enumerated. They primarily include the practice of polygamy[22] and the claim by Joseph Smith[23] that his is the only church with "true and authentic" Christianity, thereby challenging pre-existing mainstream Protestantism.[24] In many ways, Mormon history is that of the outsider challenging the establishment and encountering extraordinary resistance.

That challenge was especially problematic if, not poignant, because Mormonism sought to argue that it was true Christianity. In other words, earlier Protestant denominations were not the true way. While religious freedom was fundamental to the Founding Fathers and perhaps the core of Jeffersonian democracy, outsiders, perhaps challengers is a more effective term, have been advised to "tread warily."

Steven Waldman has suggested that Jefferson "wanted religious freedom in part because he wanted to be, religiously, free."[25] That spirit, according to Waldman, also represented Washington's and in particular Madison's approach to the practice of religion. It also was the essence of their attempt to separate church and state.[26] However, Jefferson's philosophical approach, what Waldman has described as "fury"[27] because of a belief that "Christianity was ruined almost from the start"[28] did *not*

---

21   For additional information about the historical and religious views of both the FLDS church as well as the LDS, please see the Appendix.

22   Polygamy was banned in 1890 after the prophet of the Church of Jesus Christ of Latter-Day Saints, Wilford Woodruff, claimed to have received a revelation from God banning the practice. However, many believe polygamy was banned as a condition for the admittance of Utah into the United States, rather than divine revelation.

23   The founder of the Church of Jesus Christ of Latter-Day Saints; for more information on the church, see www.lds.org.

24   *See* the Appendix for additional information on the history and beliefs of the FLDS and LDS.

25   Steve Waldman, *Founding Faith* (Random House, 2008), 85.

26   *See* Chapter Six.

27   Waldman, p. 73.

28   Waldman, p. 73.

prevent religious fundamentalism from exercising enormous power and influence.

That fundamentalism, whether in the form of early Calvinist doctrine or the Salem witch trials,[29] or in its latter day manifestations (Jerry Falwell, for example) did not brook *unconventional* religious doctrine or dogma. Their sense of *their* absolutism and righteousness (and rightness of their message and doctrine) meant that challengers, such as the Mormon Church, must be dismissed, if not ridiculed for their exclusive beliefs.

While it is well beyond the purview of this book to assign guilt or innocence regarding this complicated and sometimes violent debate, it is critical in understanding how the media has historically portrayed the Mormon Church. It is particularly crucial in examining how the media presents Mormon groups outside the traditional Mormon Church, or the "outsiders of the outsiders."

After all, whether the views expressed are fair or not, how the media approaches a particular issue is premised on perception. Precisely because the Mormon Church has been viewed as a religious "outsider" its members have been castigated for subscribing to controversial, if not odd beliefs. The religion has never been viewed as akin to mainstream Protestant denominations. Accordingly, media skepticism "translates" into media sensationalism regarding the beliefs and conduct of FLDS members. Many of the perceptions portrayed by the media have not changed since the earliest days of the church when the media and even political parties (the Republican Party) considered Mormon beliefs as one of the twin relics of barbarism, along with slavery.[30]

One of the reasons for the media's approach regarding the FLDS church—emphasizing underage sex rather than covering the underlying

---

29   While some have argued that the actual number of victims is minimal, the religious rage and absoluteness manifested cannot and should not be minimized. To suggest—as some have—that the actual burnings at the stake were minimal is to miss the essence of their importance. Arthur Miller's landmark play, *The Crucible*, brings the human element to light in an extraordinarily powerful manner. In addition, Nathaniel Hawthorne's *The Scarlet Lette"* is a classic in explaining the brutality of American religious fundamentalism.

30   1856 Republican Platform – "Resolve: That the Constitution confers upon Congress sovereign powers over the Territories of the United States for their government; and that in the exercise of this power, it is both the right and the imperative duty of Congress to prohibit in the Territories those twin relics of barbarism—Polygamy, and Slavery."

problem regarding religious extremism—is that the injured parties were members of the internal community, rather than external communities. Simply put, the danger was *restricted* to underage girls whose parents are members of the *specific* community rather than society as a whole beyond that community.

Unlike additional threats posed by religious extremism addressed in this book, the threat presented by FLDS is localized. It is community specific, rather than general. That translates into media attention highlighting the "different-ness" *rather* than accentuating the underlying story of extraordinary danger that internal members are subjected to because of religious extremism.

Simply put, the media coverage of Warren Jeffs' and the raid on the FLDS compound was limited to reporting the sensational. This suggests that if the threat is *limited* to an internal community then the scrutiny is less and the criticism more attuned to a group's sensational characteristics. Furthermore, such coverage does nothing to protect those individuals endangered by an internal community.

Ultimately, media coverage of religious extremism falls short both because it fails to properly educate the public and to engage in serious examination of the issues. The examples offered reflect a troubling reality where the media failed both the public and the individuals at risk. The dangers, long-term and short-term alike, are significant. Whichever of the four "negative" categories most aptly describes media coverage of religious extremism, the effects are largely similar. The public, regardless of whether it depends on traditional or non-traditional outlets, is largely ignorant as to religious extremism, understanding perhaps only the dangers it poses.

The same, I suggest, is largely accurate with respect to decision and policy makers who focus on the sensational while ignoring the more complicated and dangerous subtexts. Understanding those very subtexts is essential to developing a viable policy to counter religious extremism. Precisely because the media either ignores the subtexts (and its significance) or focuses solely on the sensational, the debate is largely uninformed, predicated in the main on stereotypes and assumptions. The phrase "pick your poison" is tragically apt in summarizing how the media largely covers religious extremism either mainly engaging in ignoring the essence of the threat or sensationalizing certain aspects of the threat. Both are extraordinarily dangerous and do a fundamental disservice to the public at large.

CHAPTER SIX

SEPARATING CHURCH AND STATE

INTRODUCTION

Governments struggle with how to effectively and appropriately separate church and state. In the U.S. context, the First Amendment states, "Congress shall make no law respecting an establishment of religion."[1] Freedom of religion in the United States involves two equally important clauses—the Establishment Clause and the Free Exercise Clause. The Establishment Clause prevents the government from establishing a national religion or showing preference to one religion over another. The Free Exercise Clause prevents the government from unduly interfering with the religious practice of individuals. This chapter will address the need to separate church and state. While the American reader may perceive today the separation of church and state as an issue, the fact is that in the United States separation of church and state challenges pale in comparison to other countries.

Analyzing religious extremism in the context of national security requires examining the relationship between the state and organs of religious extremism. In some cases, a state embraces religious extremism; we must examine why this occurs, and what the consequences are when it does so. In other cases, the state willfully turns a blind eye to religious extremism, thereby giving it tacit approval. This is best exemplified by states that fail to decisively punish wrongdoers who have acted in the name of religion. This is an enormous risk because it emboldens religious extremists and weakens the government's legitimacy in the eyes of society.

THE PERMANENCY OF THE STATE

One unique aspect of religious extremism is a belief that governments come and go, but religion is permanent. This point was vividly articulated in a passing conversation I had with an orthodox Jew who advocated

---

1   UNITED STATES CONSTITUTION, First Amendment.

deferments for young orthodox males from compulsory IDF service.[2] This individual argued that religion has been a mainstay for over 2,000 years, whereas the State of Israel has been in existence 60 years.[3] According to this philosophy, religion has been around "forever" whereas the nation-state, which is a recent phenomenon, should respect and honor the traditions of that which is "permanent."

The relationship between the state and organized religion in civil democratic societies is inherently complicated. There is an inevitable tension between state organs and religious institutions; that tension is at the heart of the question of whether civil law or religious law predominates in the eyes of the person of faith. While it is reasonable to assume that the person of moderate faith places civil law "above" religious law, the believer in religious extremism arguably has an alternative worldview. That alternative worldview presents the most palpable danger to contemporary, civil democratic society as religious extremists challenge the legitimacy of the state's power over them.

The traditional church/state separation discussion is predicated on the primacy of civil law over religious institutions. Those institutions cannot merely be separate from the state, but must be subservient to state law, courts, process, and directives. The essence of religious extremism is to challenge that primacy by establishing alternative regimes and institutions. This suggests the presence of a "shadow government" to which religious extremists are beholden rather than to civil institutions. The primacy argument is particularly troubling in parliamentary democracies such as Israel where governments often require the support of smaller,

---

2   According to Israeli law, males serve for three years; females for two years. According to an agreement between Israel's first Prime Minister, David Ben-Gurion, and orthodox leadership, deferments are granted to orthodox males studying in religious schools (yeshivot). Initially (late 1940s) the agreement affected hundreds; today the number of orthodox males (orthodox females are granted automatic deferment) studying in yeshivot—and therefore exempt from IDF service— numbers in the tens of thousands. It should be added that an increasing number of secular Jews are granted deferments based on medical, psychological, and personal beliefs (pacifism, conscientious objection).

3   Private conversation, in author's records.

single-issue parties to cobble a ruling coalition together. As a prominent, comparative constitutional law professor suggested,

> All coalition systems give disproportional influence to minority parties, whether they are religious or not. The government buys their support by giving them concessions, privileges and advantages.[4]

While that is undoubtedly true, what is of significance is the willingness of political leaders to include in ruling coalition's political parties not necessarily loyal to the state. While these fringe groups may not be disloyal to the state, their primary loyalty conceivably lies elsewhere. What does the state do when this split loyalty includes a belief in the preeminence of religious law over civil law?

While theocracies are undoubtedly an important field of academic study, they are beyond our purview. Not beyond our examination, however, are civil democratic societies that—for a variety of domestic political considerations—embrace religious extremists. These extremists not only view the state as illegitimate, but present a palpable threat to that nation's democracy. To thoroughly address why a state may embrace religious extremism, the issue must be viewed from the perspective of four audiences: the state, organized religion, people of faith, and secular society.

In addressing church/state relations, we must examine the relationship between state organs (law enforcement, intelligence, and security services) and religious extremists. This will significantly contribute to a better understanding of the need for the separation of church and state[5]—*not* in the "ideal" but rather in the context of the dangerous contemporary age.

ISRAEL AND SETTLERS IN THE WEST BANK AND GAZA

There may be no better example of this complicated paradox than Israel.[6] In the aftermath of the 1967 Six-Day War, Jewish settlement began in

---

4   Private email correspondence, in author's records.

5   For a greater discussion of the church/state debate, see the Appendix.

6   However, it is recommended to note the following words of wisdom written by a reader (Israeli academic) of a previous draft of this chapter: "Your main argument is that the context within which right-wing extremist settlers are operating is the overlap between State and religion in Israel. Well, of course the basic reason for the extremists' actions is biblical, but I am not sure that the above-mentioned

the West Bank and Gaza Strip based on a belief that biblical lands were part of "Greater Israel," belonging to the Jewish people.[7] Settlement activity significantly intensified after the 1973 Yom Kippur War resulting in the construction of numerous communities both in Gaza and the West Bank. In Hebrew, the communities are called "settlements;" those living on them evoking powerful emotions related to a biblical, pioneering spirit.

Numerous international law questions have been raised over the past 40 years regarding the legality and morality of these settlements. Nevertheless, the policy of Labor (left) and Likud (right) governments alike has been to consistently and actively foster the development of Jewish settlements through enormous economic, political, and military support. The wisdom of this policy is beyond this book's purview. What is relevant is the threat Jewish extremists present to the State of Israel, and the fact that despite this threat, the state continues to embrace them.

Over the course of the past 40 years, the settlement movement has been marked by an increasing lawlessness. Naturally, not all settlers or all communities are involved in criminal activity. Nevertheless, it is indisputable that an extreme faction of settlers is taking the law into their own hands. Those extremists are becoming the contemporary face, voice, and leadership of the settler movement.[8] In an effort to advance their cause, settler

---

separation will help. After all, when we talk about the settlements and the Maachazim (illegal settlements, ANG) we talk politics, we talk national security, we talk right-wing attitudes re[garding] the Arabs (regardless of religion). When the various governments, in the past, supported the settlements, I do not think it was because of separation of State and Religion. Of course, everything is helplessly interrelated".

7 While religion is obviously important to this book, the "right-ness" of religious claims by a particular religion is both beyond our purview and not an area in which I claim any expertise. To that end, interpretation of religious scripture will be left to others. It is not relevant whether particular religious-based territorial arguments are correct or not; *what is important* is that those scriptures are considered correct and that people of faith live their lives accordingly. That same argument and approach is my previously stated justification for not defining religion; for purposes of this book religion is how the person of faith defines his faith.

8 By analogy, if not by paradox, there is an interesting comparison to note: Palestinian leadership in the West Bank and Gaza Strip from 1967–1987 was relatively "docile" in reaction to the Israeli occupation; the *intifada* (1987–1993) was led by the *shabib* (youth) who came of age during the first twenty years of the occupation and over the course of six years dramatically changed the tone and tenor of both the internal Palestinian discussion and the Israeli-Palestinian relationship. While

extremists have proven that they are indiscriminate in who they attack. What is the cause? Convincing the Israeli government—Likud, Labor, or any other—that returning the West Bank, in whole or part, to Palestinian rule will involve an intolerable price to government and society alike.

There is little doubt that the settler movement, in the aftermath of disengagement from the Gaza Strip, has drawn a "line in the sand." That line is an absolute opposition to return of *any* part of the West Bank. Unlike the largely peaceful demonstrations opposing disengagement for Gaza, the assumption amongst Israeli security officials is that disengagement from the West Bank would be met forcefully, if not violently, by settlers.

As one security official commented: "[The settlers] would not shoot to kill soldiers removing settlers . . . they would only shoot at their legs."[9] Whether accurate or not, whether apocryphal or not, time will tell. That being said, its mere mention suggests an increasing recognition—and concern—regarding the potential willingness of Jewish extremists to engage in acts of terrorism and open rebellion against the state.[10]

During the past four decades, the government and the Israeli Defense Force, which acts as the executive branch in the West Bank and Gaza Strip, have had an uneasy relationship with the settler movement. Despite the fact that some settlers have clearly expressed their willingness to commit acts of violence against both Palestinian civilians and Israeli soldiers, it is clear that the relationship between the state and the settlers involves a certain level of "understanding." While sympathy is too strong a word, it is clear that there is an understanding of why the settlers took

---

undeniable that terrorist attacks were committed (both inside and outside the occupied territories) in large part by the Palestine Liberation Organization, the post 1987 terrorism is significantly different. With respect to Jewish settlers, while acts of terrorism were committed from 1967 to the present (*see* Chapter Four), the extremism and stridency that marks this generation of settler leadership is radically distinct from previous generations. The mutual, increasing extremism suggests an issue requiring the attention of policy and decision makers on both sides.

9   Private conversation, in author's records.

10   Obviously, this position is *not* universally shared; in presenting my thesis to Israeli academics and security officials, while the majority were in agreement, a minority vociferously disagreed.

the law into their own hands.[11] Perhaps the most damning evidence of the IDF's implicit authorization of the settlers' actions is the fact that the number of settlers brought to trial is disproportionately low to the number of settlers actually involved in criminal actions. These actions range from cutting down olive trees owned by Palestinians to damaging Palestinian property to attacking and killing Palestinians.

This seeming indifference to crimes committed by Israeli extremists against Palestinians has fanned the flames of an already volatile situation. While moderate settlers might be in the majority (population-wise), extremist settlers clearly determine the tone and tenor of the debate. These individuals base their actions on a combination of religious belief and the not entirely unwarranted conviction that their criminal acts will not be prosecuted. This is particularly problematic as the present generation of settlers is more extreme than their parents' generation.

Where is the state in all of this? Not only is the state failing to arrest, interrogate, and bring suspects to trial, it is failing in its fundamental obligation to impose the rule of law on all of its citizens.[12] And more

---

11   As an example, in the *immediate* aftermath of the fatal shooting of a Palestinian child by Pinchas Wallerstein (head of the West Bank Regional Council), the then Officer in Command of the IDF Central Command (West Bank), Major General Amram Mitzna (an otherwise restrained and cautious commander previously known for his sharp disagreement with then Minister of Defense Ariel Sharon regarding the First Lebanon War) stated publicly "I know Wallerstein, he is a good man."

12   It should be noted that Palestinians in the West Bank are subject both to the criminal law (trial before Military Courts) and to administrative sanctions by order of the Officer in Command (the measures include administrative detention, deportation, and house demolition); in contrast, Jewish settlers are either brought before trial in Israeli civilian courts (though living in the West Bank, they are not—for political reasons—tried in Military Courts) and subject to limited administrative sanctions that include administrative detention (Ministers' of Defense have, over the years, signed a limited number of such orders), and restraining orders (whereby an individual is prohibited from entering specific geographical areas). To date, the home of a Jewish terrorist has not been demolished (the rationale repeatedly argued before the Israeli Supreme Court sitting as the High Court of Justice with respect to demolishing Palestinian homes was to deter others from committing a similar act, meaning the rationale is not punishing the individual committing the relevant act though his family unequivocally suffered as their home was demolished; the policy was unilaterally stopped by former Prime Minister Sharon in response to an internal IDF commission which concluded the measure had not deterred Palestinians from committing acts of

than that—the state, by its failure to act, has only empowered the religious extremists it should be punishing. As such, it is fair to say that the Israeli governments, whether intended to or not, have historically been "in bed" with religious extremists in the West Bank and Gaza Strip.

FOUR AUDIENCES

So what of the four audiences mentioned earlier—the state, organized religion, people of faith, and secular society? While some lip service was paid to the dangers emanating from religious-based violence in the West Bank and Gaza, the reality is that settlers are offered a free pass. Legitimization of extremism is the indirect message sent to people of faith and secular society. Whether deliberate or not, the result was that extremist rabbis could incite and followers could act on those words.

In the context of the settler movement, the importance of this reality cannot be underestimated for moderation literally gave way to extremism over the course of the last 40 years. While the settler movement in the West Bank and Gaza Strip always had its extremist elements, the mainstream was moderate and did not view the state as illegitimate. Perhaps the de-legitimization of the state is one of the "essences" of religious extremism for it fundamentally suggests that religious law supersedes civil law. More than that, and herein lies the critical danger to personal safety and public order, it legitimizes religious-based violence as state organs are subservient to religious organs.

How does that translate into separation of religion and state in the West Bank and Gaza Strip? To answer that question, I draw on personal experience. In a number of postings in the IDF, I was at the intersection where these issues converge. Whether justified or not, the fact is that for decades the IDF has provided weapons to Jewish settlers living in the West Bank and Gaza Strip. The weapons were designated for defensive personal use, designed to enable the settlers to protect themselves against Palestinian terrorism. While it is indisputable that settlers have been targets of Palestinian terrorism, it is equally indisputable that Palestinians have been the targets of Jewish terrorism. Furthermore, and increasingly, the state (i.e., IDF soldiers) is perceived as a legitimate target by religious,

---

terrorism); to the best of my knowledge, application of this measure (applied with respect to hundreds of Palestinian homes between 1967–2004) to Jewish terrorists has never been considered, *regardless* of the crime committed.

right-wing extremists living in the West Bank who view the state as illegitimate.

When asked by senior command to recommend from which settlers previously issued weapons should be confiscated, I was invariably struck by two significant and equally disturbing facts: the random violence which typified some of the settlers and the unwillingness of the IDF, police, and Attorney General to pursue criminal charges against wrong-doers. While numerous meetings were held and various measures discussed and weighed, at the end of the day, criminal acts went unpunished. The danger, clearly, was both to potential victims and to Israeli democracy.

This last point was forcefully argued by a former senior member of the Israeli security service (ISA) in a private conversation.[13] Simply put, according to this individual, religious extremists (rabbis and followers) living in the West Bank[14] represent a "strategic threat to Israeli democracy more than Palestinian terrorism."[15] That threat—facilitated by the weapons in their possession—is extenuated by the state's unwillingness to forcefully address this issue. That is, a clear threat is unaddressed by the very officials responsible for prevention and enforcement.

In failing to punish, much less arrest, the wrongdoer, the state is sending the following message to extremists: We are afraid of you. The essence of democracy is a respect for the rule of law and punishment of the wrongdoer before a court of law predicated on the principle of "innocent until proven guilty." However, by embracing religious extremists,[16] the danger to democratic values and institutions is palpable. It is as if an additional category of citizens has been created: one that is above the law while openly and blatantly de-legitimizing the state. The state, rather than forcefully acting to protect itself against those who willfully act against the it, prefers to not engage religious extremists.

Does that mean that religious extremists are considered such a threat that, much like a schoolyard bully or neighborhood thug, pacifying or mollifying is perceived to be the preferred policy? The answer is,

---

13   Details in the author's records.

14   Post IDF disengagement from the Gaza Strip, Jewish settlers no longer live there.

15   Details in the author's records.

16   It is an open question whether religious extremism is *also* embraced or whether the embrace is limited *only* to the actor rather than the concept.

FREEDOM FROM RELIGION

tragically, yes. The only problem is, as a casual glance at the pages of history will show, the bully does not fade away. If anything, this lack of action only emboldens those who would challenge the law and the state. Add to this natural consequence the fact that religious extremists are convinced that their actions are committed in the name of a divine being.

That serving God justifies the actions of state actors epitomizes the essence of religious extremism. Killing 3,000 innocent people on a Tuesday morning is undoubtedly an evil; de-legitimizing the state presents a profoundly more significant threat to the state for it comes from within and is inherently insidious.

Separation of church and state is an elusive issue. As illustrated by the Israeli example, to not separate the two presents a clear and present danger to the state. Because religious extremists feel that the state turns a blind eye to their religious-based criminal conduct, they are understandably—and increasingly—emboldened. The lack of clear separation threatens the state as the latter becomes hesitant to fully engage the former. That however, must not justify the state's failure to fully protect against religious extremism.

Failing to do so does not serve either the state's nor the general public's fundamental interests. By blurring the line between church and state, there is an inevitable embrace; who embraces and who is embraced is an open question. However what is not an open question—rather a source of profound concern—is whether the social contract articulated by Rousseau takes a "back seat." Precisely because of the threat posed by religious extremism, the state is obligated to both articulate and implement clear boundaries between civil society and religious organs with the unequivocal understanding that the former is supreme. That is the essence of separation of church and state.

CHAPTER SEVEN

FREE EXERCISE OF RELIGION

INTRODUCTION: "FREE" EXERCISE

Does acting in the name of God justify violating the rights of others? The answer is clearly no. However, exercise of religion is critical to a person of faith. Exercising one's religion includes peaceful manifestations such as attending religious services, wearing symbols associated with religion,[1] conducting oneself in accordance with religious guidelines,[2] and decorating one's house in accordance with one's faith.[3] Yet, action in the name of religion is not boundless.[4]

Under the current legal structure in the United States, religious *beliefs* are absolutely protected, but *conduct* in furtherance of those beliefs may be regulated. For example, a state may prohibit certain illegal conduct[5] and may require others, including paying taxes, despite a claim generated by the free exercise clause.[6] However, such regulations may not be religiously motivated for the state cannot create a law specifically designed

---

1   A cross, Star of David, headscarf are prime examples; as a teenager I wore a Star of David as a symbol of Jewish identity but not as a symbol of religious belief, which raises the legitimate question of whether Islamic women who wear a headscarf are doing so for cultural-religious reasons or ones of religious belief; it is my understanding that Jewish women who wear headscarves do so exclusively because of religious dictated modesty and not "cultural identity" reasons.

2   Examples would range from observing dietary restrictions (fasting during Ramadan, abstaining from meat during Lent, not eating pork) to not driving on the Sabbath, to making the pilgrimage to Mecca (*ha'j*).

3   Decorating a Christmas tree, lighting a Hanukkah menorah are prime examples, although *not* all who employ these traditions do so for religious reasons; see comment in above footnote regarding cultural-religious motivations.

4   *See, e.g., Employment Division v. Smith*, 494 U.S. 872 (1990) (upholding the law prohibiting the peyote during religious ceremonies).

5   *See, e.g., Reynolds v. U.S.*, 98 U.S. 145 (1878) (upholding a law forbidding polygamy despite the claim that it was required for religion).

6   *See, e.g., U.S. v. Lee*, 455 U.S. 252 (1982) (rejecting the challenge by Amish individuals who claimed that the law requiring that they obtain social security numbers and pay social security taxes violated their religious beliefs.

to target a religion.[7] The courts determine whether the law presents a purposeful interference with religious exercise. If it does, the law must pass a strict scrutiny test;[8] if the law merely presents an incidental burden on exercise of religion, the law must pass a balancing test similar to rational basis standards.[9]

While the courts have set standards for specific state interest in promotion of state law, our question is whether the exercise of religion threatens state security. If so, can the state step in to limit that free exercise—and when can it step in? Ultimately, this chapter argues that the law must allow a state to step in earlier to limit conduct that threatens security, despite the fact that it is performed as "free" exercise of religion.

THREATS TO THE STATE

The exercise of religion need not *automatically* be interpreted as a threat to national security, far from it. That said, there is little doubt today that religious symbols, or what are interpreted as religious symbols, are forcing decision makers to determine whether wearing certain symbols *may* threaten national security. Certain conduct, despite the argument that it is performed as part of the free exercise of religion, threatens security, and therefore poses a threat to the state. However, *how* the threat is defined is a complicated debate. Only after a threat is defined can the state determine the steps that need to be taken to protect itself from the threat.

Determining if religious exercise poses a danger to the state requires a threat analysis. This analysis requires asking the following questions: What is the threat the state faces? Is it an actual, real threat or just a perceived threat? When will that threat be carried out? Answering the last question requires determining both the imminence of the threat and its viability.

Imminent threats are those that are to be shortly conducted; as an example, a "hot" intelligence report suggests that a bomb will

---

7   *See, e.g., Church of the Lukumi Babalu v. Hialeah,* 508 U.S. 520 (1993) (holding that if the law's purpose is specifically to infringe on religious practice, it must pass a strict scrutiny test; an ordinance designed to ban only a particular kind of animal sacrifice targeted one religion did not pass strict scrutiny).

8   *Id.*

9   *See, Employment Division v. Smith,* 494 U.S. 872 (1990) (upholding the law prohibiting the peyote during religious ceremonies).

be detonated *tomorrow* at 9:15 a.m. at a domestic terminal at JFK airport.

Foreseeable threats are those that will be carried out *within a year* and are therefore more distant than an imminent threat. For example, a foreseeable threat includes valid intelligence that indicates that terrorists will shortly begin bringing explosives onto airplanes in liquid substances.

Long-range threats are specific threats that may reach fruition at an unknown time; for example, terrorist's training with no operational measure specifically planned would fit in this category.

Uncertain threats constitute those that invoke general fears of insecurity. As a result of train bombings in England and Spain, travelers in the United States might potentially or conceivably feel insecure riding trains without bolstered security. This would be true regardless of whether there is valid intelligence indicating terrorists intend to start targeting trains in the United States.

The more real and imminent the threat is to the state, the greater the state's justification for limiting certain conduct associated with that threat even if performed in the furtherance of religious belief. The types of potentially threatening religious conduct vary widely depending on the specific religion. Therefore, the threat must be examined specifically and sensitively to determine if and when a state has a justifiable right to limit that conduct.

The types of conduct examined below include clearly illegal conduct which presents an immediate threat and therefore does not enjoy First Amendment protection. This conduct cannot be justified under a defense of free exercise of religion (e.g., Paul Hill). However, conduct which involves criminal activity and puts individuals in harm's way, raises crucial questions as to *when* a state may step in to prevent and/or prosecute criminal conduct performed in the exercise of religion (e.g., the FLDS). Finally, non-violent conduct in furtherance of the exercise of religious belief is only banned after the state has perceived a threat, though not necessarily reaching the level of national security. Perhaps this is best described as an exercise of unnecessary governmental overreach (e.g., the headscarf).

WHEN MAY/MUST THE STATE ACT—THE FLDS

While illegal conduct in the name of faith is clearly unprotected and not justified by the affirmative defense of "free exercise," when can the state step in to prevent and/or prosecute such conduct? For members of the FLDS faith, free exercise of religion includes the mandated practice of plural marriage.[10] Religious leaders, particularly Warren Jeffs, maintain ultimate authority over church members requiring certain criminal conduct as part of membership. As one member noted, "our foundation is obedience, acceptance of church authority and a belief in one-man rule."[11]

Shortly after Warren Jeffs's ascension to the position of prophet, his admonitions became commandments from God; disobeying meant excommunication and eternal damnation.[12] Jeffs' laws extended beyond the traditional practice of religion, as members were required to discard their televisions and radios.[13] Jeffs told his members that extracurricular activities that took away from family were ungodly; immediately there-after, as an example, all the basketball equipment in the community was removed.[14] Furthermore, Jeffs demanded that members of his congregation destroy their secular books.[15]

Perhaps most relevant and critical to this discussion is that Jeffs insisted on having underage girls marry much older men. To that end, Jeffs required his daughter marry a 34-year-old man the day after her 15th birthday.[16] Jeffs' daughter Teresa had written in her diary, "the Lord blessed me to go forward in marriage July 27, 2006, the day after I turned 15 years old."[17] However, when subpoenaed to testify in court, Teresa denied ever being married and filed complaints against her court-ordered

---

10   The belief in polygamy, "plural marriage" as it was termed, comes from a revela-
        tion in the Doctrine and Covenants where Joseph Smith said that plural marriage
        was to become part of religious practice again, as it had been in the past. Members
        of the Church of Jesus Christ of Latter-Day Saints (LDS) reject this practice.

11   Tom Zoellner, "Rulon Jeffs: patriarch, president, prophet for polygamy," *Salt Lake
        Tribune*, June 28, 1998.

12   Brooke Adams, "Warren Jeffs profile: Thou shalt obey," *Salt Lake Tribune*, March
        14, 2004, at http://www.sltrib.com/polygamy/ci_3805407.

13   *Id.*

14   *Id.*

15   *Id.*

16   *Available at* http://www.dallasnews.com/sharedcontent/dws/dn/latestnews/storie
        s/060408dntexpolygamists.59202c61.html.

17   Reports: Jeffs marries underage daughter to adult, *Salt Lake Tribune*, July 19, 2008,
        at http://www.ksl.com/?nid=148&sid=3808154&autostart=y.

attorney after being removed from the polygamist community, the Yearning for Zion Ranch, along with 400 other children.[18] Such a reaction was common amongst Jeffs' followers. One woman defended the fact that she let her 12-year-old daughter marry Jeffs; she told the court she would not prevent contact between her daughter and the man accused of being involved in underage marriages.[19]

Warren Jeffs did not ask his followers to sacrifice their own lives or kill others; he did, however demand of his followers that their underage daughters marry grown men and engage in full sexual relations with them. In other words, in the name of free exercise of religion, Jeffs demanded of his followers that their daughters be endangered, physically and emotionally. While this is not akin to tragedies such as Jonestown[20] and the Heaven's Gate cult,[21] the control that religious extremists' clergy—such as a Warren Jeffs—exert over their congregants must not be underestimated.

Limitation of the free exercise of religion in respect to FLDS poses an important question in the larger context. FLDS presents no perceived or actual threat to the national security of the United States. In fact it would be an irresponsible "stretch" to argue that Warren Jeffs endangers the national security of the U.S. Furthermore, it would be a similarly irresponsible claim to suggest that Jeffs' intention (pre-incarceration) was to endanger America. It was his intention to ensure the faithfulness of his congregants, which included religiously ordained marriage between FLDS members resulting in forced sexual relations between minors and adults. For that, Jeffs was convicted of two counts of being an accomplice to rape of a child.

FLDS practice *clearly* presents a threat to *certain* members, in particular to minor girls in danger from the combination of underage marriage and

---

18   *Id.*

19   Texas judge says 14-year-old allegedly wed to polygamist leader Jeffs must go to foster care, http://www.washingtontimes.com/news/2008/aug/20/teen-tied-to-sect-put-in-foster-care/.

20   In November of 1978, Jim Jones the leader of The People's Temple cult, told his 912 followers to drink a deadly cocktail of cyanide, sedatives, and tranquilizers to preserve their church. Jones apparently shot himself in the head shortly after.

21   Cult leader Marshall Applegate convinced followers that the only way to reach the "Next Level" was to commit suicide. Starting on March 27, 1997, 39 members of the cult committed suicide in three successive groups over a three-day period.

subsequent forced sexual relations. That practice endangers an otherwise *unprotected* class; accordingly the free exercise of religion is extraordinarily problematic. It is also dangerous.

Determining *when* and how much the free exercise must be curtailed presents enormous challenges to law enforcement. In the American paradigm, the decision to *limit* the free exercise of religion is fraught with danger, constitutional complexity, and tension. The traditional argument is that "probable cause" demands sufficient evidence be available *prior* to state intervention. However, the present danger that underage girls are exposed to, devoid of parental protection, suggests an urgent need to re-articulate that standard with respect to a *specific* threat posed by this exercise of religious extremism.

The test for determining when and how to limit exercise is predicated on the previously addressed threat analysis. FLDS religious practice is a threat that places a particular population in harm's way, and that harm is exacerbated because it is theologically predicated. Given that plural marriage is part of FLDS dogma and that FLDS leaders order minor girls to marry older men, this harm is definitely "foreseeable." As this is a known threat to unprotected girls, the state has a responsibility to step in.

Individual states struggle with the issue of FLDS members and leaders. On July 26, 1953, Arizona state law enforcement raided the polygamist community of Short Creek, removing 263 children. Even though all of the women who had left the community with their children were put into foster homes for two years, they all resumed their polygamist lives.[22] The raid became a rallying point for the FLDS church, a tale of the test of faith; "Remember Short Creek" became a motto among polygamists.[23] "The backlash drove a governor from office and discouraged officials from taking action against the practice of polygamy for half a century. It also left a traumatic imprint in the collective mind of a community that has withdrawn from an outside world it views as evil."[24]

---

22   Carole Mikita, "Historian compares Texas raid to 1953 raid on Short Creek," KSL.com, April 9, 2008, *available at* http://www.ksl.com/index.php?nid=572&sid=3047173.

23   *Id.*

24   Gary Tuchman and Amanda Townsend, "A Dark History Repeats for Religious Sect," CNN, *available at* http://www.cnn.com/2008/CRIME/04/10/polygamist.towns/index.html.

Some draw a parallel from Short Creek to the 2008 raid on the Yearning for Zion Ranch in Eldorado, Texas.[25] In 2008, police raided the Texas ranch and removed over 400 children from their parents after receiving an anonymous phone call from someone claiming to be a minor who had been sexually abused inside the FLDS compound; the phone call was later determined to be a hoax.[26] The Texas Supreme Court found that child welfare officials had overstepped their authority in determining that the children were at risk and ordered them released.[27] Texas officials said that they would move forward on a case-by-case basis, seeking to remove children from their parents for individual cases of abuse, a much slower process.[28]

Ultimately, practices such as child rape and plural marriage present a viable foreseeable threat to individuals. Therefore, the state must step in sooner to prevent and subsequently prosecute criminal action conducted in the name of religious extremism. The question of how to step in is fraught with difficulty and fear of backlash, but it is a difficulty that must be directly addressed. Even if it clashes with the free exercise clause of the U.S. Constitution, states must act as they bear ultimate responsibility for citizen protection.

That obligation is magnified when the particular population group in question is otherwise unprotected and particularly vulnerable because of the religious beliefs of those who should be most concerned about their welfare and safety—their parents. The lower level of intermediate scrutiny should therefore apply with respect to the free exercise of religion that directly results in child brides and forced sexual relations.

THE DANGER OF GOVERNMENTAL OVERREACH—THE HEADSCARF

While illegal, violent, and criminal conduct is clearly not protected under the constitution, even when committed in the name of faith, what happens when a state targets non-violent religious conduct, in the name

---

25 Geoffrey Fattah, *Parallels to Short Creek Raid in 1953 are Pointed Out*, DESERET NEWS, April 10, 2008, *available at* http://www.deseretnews.com/article/1,5143,695269050,00.html; *see also* footnote 22 on the previous page.

26 Miguel Bustillo and Nicholas Riccardi, *FLDS Raid Appears to have Backfired*, L.A. TIMES, May 31, 2008, *available at* http://articles.latimes.com/2008/may/31/nation/na-polygamist31.

27 *Id.*

28 *Id.*

of a threat to the state? The debate surrounding the wearing of head-scarves by Muslim women has become a critical question when discussing contemporary free exercise of religion. Why do Muslim women wear the headscarf, and why do some nations, such as France and Turkey, feel threatened by it?[29] Is this threat real, viable, imminent, and thus worthy of state limitation, or is such a limitation an example of government overreach and thus an unnecessary infringement on a fundamental right?

According to the Qu'ran and the traditions of the prophet Muhammad, Muslim women should guard their modesty, should not display beauty and adornments in public except that which may ordinarily appear, such as the face and hands.[30] To that end, wearing a headscarf, intended to cover up a woman's hair, meets the modesty requirement. The interpretation of this edict from the Qu'ran varies widely; while some claim that the headscarf is a mandate of Islam, others claim that such a strict interpretation is unwarranted.[31] Regardless of the answer, women choose to wear the headscarf for many reasons including the belief that it is a mandate, the personal desire to display modesty, the practical desire to focus attention on inner beauty, and the desire to show that they are different, a Muslim.[32] Of course, not all Muslim women choose to wear the headscarf.

For those who do wear the scarf, what is the state's concern? States have various interpretations and subsequent applications. In France, wearing a headscarf is banned in public school, as part of a law prohibiting wearing conspicuous religious symbols in the classroom.[33] The headscarf is seen as a threat to French society for it is understood to emphatically declare religious identity. The visible Muslim presence has therefore added a pronounced religious dimension to increasing French concerns

---

29   For additional discussion regarding the headscarf in Turkey, see the Appendix.

30   *See* "The Hijab," ISLAM 101, *available at* http://www.islam101.com/women/hijabfaq.html, discussing the Qu'ran, Chapter 24, verses 30–31.

31   *See* Brian Rokus, "Muslim Women: My Headscarf is Not a Threat," CNN, *available at* http://www.cnn.com/2007/WORLD/meast/08/21/hijab.godswarriors/index.html.

32   *See* Amina Hernandez, "Why I Wear a Headscarf," *available at* http://www.islamonline.net/servlet/Satellite?c=Article_C&cid=1154235126891&pagename=Zone-English-Discover_Islam%2FDIELayout.

33   *See* "French Scarf Ban Comes into Force," *available at* http://news.bbc.co.uk/2/hi/europe/3619988.stm.

regarding immigration and integration. Further, the headscarf is seen as a political symbol that threatens the secular worldview and, for some, even "embraces Islamic extremism."[34] In contrast, Muslim girls in Britain are free to wear the headscarf, while in Germany the debate over the issue continues.[35]

Parallel to the French concerns, perhaps the most striking recent debate over the headscarf has occurred in Turkey. Turkey, a secular state, has traditionally banned wearing the headscarf in public institutions which the European Court of Human Rights upheld in 2005.[36] Leyla Sahin, a Muslim student at Istanbul University, challenged the headscarf ban after being excluded from class for wearing a headscarf.[37] Sahin claimed that the ban discriminated against her and denied her right to an education.[38] The court held that the law was consistent with the European Convention on Human Rights and was a reasonable measure to protect Turkey's secular society. The Court considered both the impact on those who wear it as a symbol as well as the effect it has on those who choose not to wear it.[39]

In 2008, two constitutional amendments were passed that would lift the headscarf ban on university campuses. However, this was met with protest and political turmoil. Secular Turks questioned lifting the ban that had been imposed to protect secularism in Turkey; others feared that lifting the ban marked a step that would "encourage radical Islamic circles in Turkey, accelerate movement towards a state founded on religion, lead to further demands against the spirit of the republic."[40] Ultimately, the constitutional court in Turkey upheld the headscarf ban, ruling that the amendments were unlawful because "secularism was the unalterable principle of the Turkish Republic."[41]

---

34   See "Q&A: Muslim Headscarf," available at http://news.bbc.co.uk/2/hi/europe/ 3328277.stm.

35   Ibid.

36   See Leyla Sahin v. Turkey, ECHR 44774/98 (2005).

37   Id.

38   Id.

39   Id.

40   http://news.bbc.co.uk/2/hi/europe/7230075.stm.

41   Brendan O'Malley, Turkey: Headscarf ban re-imposed, UNIVERSITY WORLD NEWS, June 8, 2008, available at http://www.universityworldnews.com/article.php? story=20080606083302196.

In spite of court decisions addressing the legality of laws denying Muslim women the right to the wear the headscarf, I suggest the issue is politically rather than legally driven. Borrowing from themes suggested by Christian Smith in *American Evangelicalism*,[42] I suggest that the headscarf raises important questions regarding absolutism, accommodation, and vibrancy; *absolutism* as in the absolutism of belief; *accommodation* as in whether religion accommodates modernity; and *vibrancy* as identified by church attendance. In the absolutism, accommodation, and vibrancy discussion, the headscarf represents a critical meeting point. Religion and culture, expression of religious faith, tensions between traditional religion and modernity and government apprehensions regarding the "unknown" inherent to religious belief intersect here.

Absolutism is traditionally associated with an "all or nothing" approach; in the religion debate it suggests that no compromise is possible. It is another way of stating "my God is the Truth" (capital T critical to the believer) and all other gods are dismissed. However, absolutism can also be a secular quality. In the scarf debate it suggests that regimes banning the scarf have an absolute belief in the threat it poses. Otherwise why ban it?

This leads to the accommodation question: Should the state not accommodate how individuals wish to practice their faith? Or, on the other hand, should faith accommodate the state? How faith is expressed is inherent to how it is practiced. Meaning if modesty is important to the tenets of particular faith "A," then how that modesty is conveyed and implemented is critical to the person of faith "A."

Whether the state chooses to accommodate that belief in "A" and allow conduct in furtherance of that belief depends on a variety of circumstances and considerations. Those considerations include: perceived public and individual safety, discrimination against a particular faith, cultural and societal values, political realities, current events, and geopolitical calculations.

Ultimately, does "A" face an impermissible burden if exercise of that faith is limited? The answer is "perhaps" but that is the price of the social contract. There are no absolute rights. So, if accommodation is inherent to civil democratic societies on multiple levels, then the obvious question is when should "A" accommodate "B" (other faiths) and "C" (non-believers

---

42   Christian Smith, *American Evangelicalism: Embattled and Thriving*, UNIVERSITY OF CHICAGO PRESS, 1998.

in all faiths) with respect to the headscarf. Simply put, if the headscarf makes "B" and "C" uncomfortable, then the government may be "right" to limit, if not ban, its use. On the other hand, perhaps "B" and "C" do not understand what the scarf means and their reaction is ignorance-based and may be facilitated (wittingly or not) by government leaders interested (for political reasons) to foment fear and anxiety.

This leads us to vibrancy; while church attendance is an oft-cited barometer of religious vibrancy, I have always found it a statistic of dubious significance. Were all my fellow congregants at services in Ann Arbor, Michigan[43] vibrant in their faith? I would suggest many attended services, in particular during the High Holidays (Rosh Hashanah and Yom Kippur) for a variety of reasons including cultural identification, social engagement, and perceived obligation to others. That is not to dismiss the legitimacy of their attendance. Not in the least. But it is intended to suggest that attendance in and of itself does not suggest nor prove vibrancy. The same, I offer, is true with respect to the wearing of the scarf. Simply put, it may well be a showing of cultural pride rather than religious vibrancy.

If wearing a scarf is a sign of vibrancy, extolling and taking pride in one's religion, then identifying the harm or threat is difficult to gauge. Smith suggests that threat must also be examined from the "internal" perspective; that is, the threat a particular religion feels from the external world. While Smith suggests this with respect to American evangelicals, perhaps the same argument can be made with respect to Muslim women. That is, the wearing of the headscarf is both cultural-religious identification and a means of expressing their concern with threats with respect to the outside world.

While it is clear that the headscarf has significance, what is not clear is whether it warrants the extraordinary attention it receives. If it is a religious or cultural statement, not intended as, nor proved to be, a violent exercise, or incitement toward extremism, what is the possible threat? Perhaps the state *assumes* based on events of recent years that it *symbolizes* religious extremism that potentially endangers the state. The suggestion that something *symbolic* presents a danger to the state requires an analysis significantly different than that appropriate to the clear danger posed by Paul Hill.

---

43   Where I was raised.

For Turkey, and states with similar views, the headscarf presents a threat, not to national security, but to the Secular Republic. Accordingly, the state has passed laws to limit that threatening exercise by banning the wearing of the headscarf in certain milieus. Considering the threat analysis suggested by this book, does that make the scarf a real, actual threat warranting limitation? No. The threat is perceived, not imminent, which can only be characterized as, at best, uncertain. However much the headscarf is *perceived* to pose a threat, it is not a threat to national security, and it does not equate the *actual imminent* harm posed by an individual such as Paul Hill. Therefore, a complete ban on a non-violent religious exercise such as the headscarf suggests classic over-reaction,[44] and is unnecessary.

NECESSARY LIMITS

Ultimately, while the current legal framework allows for judicial over-sight into laws that have an effect on free exercise, the state must not acquiesce to criminal conduct because it is performed in the furtherance of a religious belief. If a state places a burden on free exercise of religion, such as banning polygamy and child rape, those laws must be enforced. While FLDS acts under the guise of the free exercise of religion, the state must be allowed to act to limit this exercise if there is either a threat to individuals or society as a result of that exercise. However, a state must be careful not to engage in governmental overreach. Exercise, such as wearing of a headscarf, does not present an actionable, viable, imminent, or foreseeable threat to the security of the state; therefore, there is no need to ban it under the premise of this book. To do so is to unnecessarily engage in excess and to indiscriminately categorize all religious conduct as a threat. While religious extremist conduct must be limited, there is no need to do so with respect to religious conduct that poses no threat. To do so not only violates fundamental rights, it has the unfortunate side-effect of driving believers of a peaceful faith into the waiting arms of the extremists.

---

44   Amos N. Guiora, "Transnational Comparative Analysis of Balancing Competing Interests in Counterterrorism," *Temple International & Comparative Law Journal*, 20 TEMP. INT'L & COMP. L.J.

CHAPTER EIGHT

CULTURAL CONSIDERATIONS AND
THE PRICE OF RELIGIOUS LIBERTY

INTRODUCTION

There is a price for religious liberty. In the desire to protect the individuals' rights to pursue separate opinions and beliefs, we accept the possibility that some of those opinions and beliefs will result in harm to others and society at large. Prime Minister Rabin paid this price with his life; similarly, underage girls in the FLDS Church were violated, and will most likely continue to be abused. These are perhaps some of the most dramatic examples of the harmful effects of religious extremism.

It is easy to say that religious speech that encourages murder and rape is limitable. But what about cultural practices offensive from the majority's perspective, but not inherently harmful? What about those that are harmful? Cultural relativism is the idea that beliefs and conduct should be understood in terms of the individual speaker or actor's culture. This view suggests that all beliefs are equally valid and truth itself is relative, depending on the situation and environment. The alternative is universalism, the theory that some values cross cultural lines, and should be applied to all individuals.

Cultural relativism should be viewed on a sliding scale. For the vast majority of cases, society must tolerate practices even when it finds them distasteful, for that is the price of both religious and secular liberty. Some might be offended by the notion of parents arranging their children's marriages; yet so long as the children are adults and are not forced into anything, there is no harm to them or society. Yet, as the mores and norms of some cultures become more and more extreme, society has a greater obligation to enforce universal values to protect the life and health of others.

FEMALE GENITAL CUTTING

Mainstream society, a problematic term that implies judgment on those outside the "mainstream," needs to understand that certain practices are essential to how others practice their belief system. In the ideal, how others practice or manifest their beliefs is of no concern to others. That said, some practices endanger the individual and therefore the state has an obligation to prevent otherwise free exercise of religion.

In the religious paradigm, the question is whether practices are acceptable, even though harm to individuals is possible, because they are so important to the practitioners. A clear example is female genital cutting (FGC),[1] a practice whereby the female external genitalia is partially or totally cut away. It is practiced predominantly in 28 African countries, some Middle Eastern countries, Indonesia, Malaysia, Pakistan, and India. Immigrant groups in Australia, Canada, New Zealand, the U.S., and other European nations also practice it. While the groups who practice FGC consider it an important part of their cultural and religious heritage, there are numerous physical complications that can arise from the procedure.

The free exercise of religion is not a license to harm others. Additionally, cultural traditions cannot be respected if they are merely a justification of harm to others, even if the practice is considered important and legitimate to particular groups. In the vast majority of cases, FGC involves children, not adult women. If such actions would be considered child abuse in any other context, why are they not considered child abuse when conducted in the context of an internal society, predicated on religious extremism?

The issue of religious practices deemed harmful by society must be viewed from the perspective of the practicing group before it is deemed harmful, much less illegal. That is, cultural and religious relativism must be taken into account. Doing so requires asking why certain practices are so important for particular groups. In doing so, one of many questions is whether a particular practice is so essential to a particular group that without it, the belief system is fundamentally impacted to the extent that they cannot practice their religion.

In examining the limits of religious conduct it is essential to discuss how different religions define conduct essential to their faith and belief system. Wearing a skullcap is discussed in the Old Testament; it is a means by which male Jews express their religious faith. The same is true for the wearing of phylacteries when praying, or growing beards. The examples

---

1   While female genital cutting is practiced among Muslim groups, it is more of a cultural phenomenon; *see* http://forwoman.gov/faq/female-genital-cutting.cfm.

of physical manifestations of religious faith are essential to people of faith and represent non-harmful conduct prescribed by religious tenets for thousands of years. Similarly, attending church on Sundays for Protestants or daily Mass for Catholics, and praying five times a day for Muslims is essential to how hundreds of millions of people express their faith daily, or weekly, from generation to generation.

There are obvious pitfalls in discussing religious-based conduct because the legitimate question is whether the conduct that is ascribed to religion is truly religious or simply cultural. While the distinction may be intellectually interesting, in reality it may be irrelevant. The actor generally ascribes conduct to religion, and so whether the anthropological roots are cultural or religious has no true relevancy. The person acting genuinely believes that as a matter of faith, he/she must act in a particular manner.

HONOR KILLINGS

The topic of honor killings is intensely troubling and personal for me. In 1993, while serving as a Judge in the Gaza Strip Military Court, I was assigned an honor killing case. That was my first, and only, experience with a crime that literally defies description. While civilian murder is not a crime traditionally brought before a Military Court,[2] this particular case involved a suspected informant for the General Security Services who along with his brother and mother were accused of murdering their sister suspected of dishonoring the family.

The following details are overwhelmingly graphic, but the issue needs to be fully understood before it is discussed. In the case before me, the victim had been accused of shaming her family by having sexual relations with a man before marriage. Initially, her brothers sought to beat her to death. When she survived this brutal beating, the mother ordered her sons to tie their sister's legs to two separate beds. According to testimony, the victim resisted to the point of exhaustion, at which point the mother ordered the two brothers to begin pulling the beds in opposite directions. At the mother's constant urging, the two brothers were ultimately successful in dismembering their sister. The process took hours and the victim suffered horribly before her tragic death.

What made the case particularly chilling was both the dispassionate manner in which all three testified and the utter lack of remorse they

---

2   Non-security crimes were usually brought before a Palestinian court.

expressed when given the opportunity. The reality is that honor killings are not rare and isolated; they are undeniably frequent. While they do not all involve the sort of horrific details described above, it is clear they are happening. Furthermore, like many crimes that occur behind closed doors, statistics are likely inaccurate.

The real question is to what extent society is willing to tolerate behavior based on principles of cultural relativism. Fifty years ago in the United States, society turned a blind eye to domestic violence. So long as these beatings were not "extreme," society was willing to tolerate them. Is it possible that societies, which have long since abandoned their informal stance of turning a blind eye to domestic violence, are unwilling to address violence in "other" cultural groups? Are they ascribing indifference as respect?

The easy answer is that when harm is caused to another, religious conduct is no longer to be tolerated, nor used as justification. Yet much of this violence occurs within the confines of the home, beyond the sight of the state. States should become more proactive, given the knowledge that in some communities the possibility of certain types of violence is much higher. The state must not respond only after the most horrific crimes have occurred. There must be deterrent and proactive action.

What had this woman done to earn such a cruel fate? Accused of having acted immorally, she had dishonored her family. For that, according to extremist Islamic beliefs, she must be killed. Whether the foundation for the conduct is religious or cultural or an intertwining of the two is not clear. While modesty has different meanings in different cultures, no religious text explicitly calls for the killing of someone who acted immodestly. Yet, in certain cultures, that is exactly what occurs. Interpretation by extremists of religious text grants license to family members to kill a family member who has shamed the family.

What is particularly troubling is the acquiescence of the community; or perhaps, more accurately, the community support for the act. Even more troubling than that is the direct role played by parents, and in particular, mothers. Mothers are traditionally considered the nurturing parent; yet examples exist suggesting the mother's direct role in the murder of the very child to whom she gave birth.

This is, by all standards, unlawful behavior that should be severely punished. When it is not, it reflects nothing but community support for the crime. When the community and its legal and judicial infrastructure knowingly and willingly turn a blind eye to murder in the name of religion, they are complicit in murder. The tension is palpable. Actually, tragically, it is not palpable because religious extremism in communities where honor killings are accepted is trumping civil society defined as respect for the rule of law.

In addressing honor killings, it is critical to ask where "mainstream society" is. The point was poignantly brought home when I was in Canada in December 2007. According to media reports, a Muslim father stabbed his teenage daughter to death—her crime was wearing tight jeans and having a non-Islamic boyfriend. He stabbed her repeatedly in the comfort and safety of his own home when she returned from an evening out. While the role of the mother was not clear, it was obvious from the media reports that she was home, and that she failed to intervene to save her child.

It is also clear that the media was unable to define the crime properly. Rather than calling it what it is, an honor killing, the media sought to address it in the context of "political correctness" and phrase it in terms of a violent father with anger management issues. Completely ignored was the fact that the father was acting in accordance with an extreme view of Islam that would justify his actions. Whether this omission was made out of respect to religious sensibilities or in an effort not to offend cultural sensitivities is irrelevant. The fact is that this trend cannot be addressed until society recognizes it for what it is—an act of violence premised on extremist religious justification.

In seeking to address the issue with policymakers and academics, most were unwilling to address the greater issue surrounding the murder. Rather, their response is best summarized as claiming that these things are "internal, religious, cultural, and societal matters." This attitude goes to the heart of the issue; religious extremism is not an internal matter and must no longer enjoy *de facto* immunity because the state wants to respect different beliefs of its citizens.

JUSTICE YITZHAK ZAMIR

In the course of writing this book, I was fortunate to meet and speak with hundreds of people, both off the record and on. One of the most important and compelling interviews was with retired Justice Yitzhak Zamir of the Israel Supreme Court. Professor Zamir, who prior to his appointment to the Court served as Israel's Attorney General, articulated the notion that ideological offenses are different from traditional crimes,[3] and therefore must be considered more dangerous. The "ideological criminal" does not benefit financially or personally from his crimes. In the Israeli model, those acting in the name of Judaism commit the ideological offenses Zamir refers to.

While former Prime Minister Shamir termed members of the 1980s Jewish underground "good boys," Zamir suggests an additional perspective. The actions of ideological offenders and their offences cannot be divorced from the support they receive from different publics. Those publics break down into different categories, some of them chillingly similar to the groups relevant to honor crimes. Chillingly is used deliberately because there is, at least, a doubly chilling effect in play with respect to religious extremism. The first is the internal community's failure to condemn acts of violence committed in the name of religion; the second is the larger public's tacit support.

To suggest that violent acts such as honor killings are merely an internal matter is disingenuous. It invites the next stabbing of a young woman believed to have violated her family's honor. Whether the core belief in this form of punishment is religious or cultural is not critical to the discussion. While the murderer may believe his or her actions are grounded in religious text, there is little doubt that cultural considerations are also relevant to the decision to kill the wayward family member. I suggest that the two are intertwined; in the context of Zamir's articulation of ideological offenses, the combination is deadly. This is particularly exacerbated when mainstream society and the media choose, for all practical purposes, to ignore an extraordinarily problematic reality.

This raises an issue of overriding importance: What is the cause of this fear to arrest, interrogate, and bring to trial individuals acting in the name of religion? The hesitation includes the judiciary which, when given the opportunity to impose stiff sentences on ideological offenders, fails to do so. The punishments received by members of the Jewish underground were deemed by Zamir (as Attorney General) to be sufficiently lenient that he appealed the sentences to the Supreme Court. The Court denied the appeal; from his perspective an important opportunity was missed *both* to penalize the wrongdoers commensurate with

---

3   Zamir defines "traditional crime" as both criminal activity including robbery, rape, and murder, and crimes of government corruption. With respect to the latter, Zamir suggests that given the dramatic increase in corruption-related cases in Israel, this crime must be viewed with great seriousness but argues that ideological crimes are, nevertheless, more dangerous.

proportionality principles and to "send an educational and public message" to the offenders, their supporters (passive and active alike), and the general public. The significance is clear: religious extremism or perhaps more accurately, actions on behalf of religious extremism are tolerated, if not excused by mainstream society and its institutions.

The discussion regarding punishment—when and how much—ultimately depends on a confluence of circumstances that includes relevant clauses of the criminal code, the meeting of applicable evidentiary standards, prosecutorial discretion, determination of guilt or innocence, and sentencing either by a bench or jury trial. How the public views crimes committed in the context of religious extremism undoubtedly impacts the sentences imposed. That question forces us to confront public tolerance, if not acceptance, of violence in the name of religious extremism. Otherwise, how else can a long list of violent acts be explained?

The price of religious liberty is critical to the freedom of religion discussion. If the price includes acts of violence that largely go unpunished, then religious freedom must be curtailed. Even if the religious conduct is cloaked in culture rather than pure religion, the results are largely the same. What Justice Zamir refers to as ideological offenses result in serious crime. If that were not enough, the lack of a firm, institutionalized, and consistent response by state institutions only serves to reinforce what I have termed elsewhere as immunity for religious extremism. While highly problematic, it is a concept that clearly deserves careful examination.

What is particularly troubling is what Justice Zamir refers to as the connecting of dots. In other words, there is a historical pattern of religious extremist violence that in the main has gone unpunished. More than that, particularly in the West Bank, law enforcement officials have not reacted with the full weight of the law. The Karp Report, authored by then Deputy State Legal Advisor Yehudit Karp, carefully described a consistent pattern of non-enforcement by the authorities with respect to settler violence against innocent Palestinians. The reasons are fairly obvious—ranging from identification with the settlers to fears regarding future acts of violence. Be that as it may, the result is clearly damage to the rule of law. In essence, that is the price paid for not acting forcefully against religious extremism.

On the other hand, people of faith, whether acting in the context of religion or culture, have the right to express their opinions. Over-reacting is as dangerous as under-reacting. To that end, I met with senior officials in the State Attorney's office in order to discuss *legal policy* with respect both to incitement and settler violence. After all, the price for liberty, as well as religious and cultural freedom is critical to the discussion. The conversation was extraordinarily candid, forthcoming, and important in the context of the book's thesis.

It is also relevant to how prosecutors and courts should address honor killings. When I asked Zamir, "Have we learned anything from Rabin's assassination?" his answer was, "theoretically, yes, practically, no." That was the essence of my conversation with the State Attorney's office. While there have been changes in the criminal code, the reality is that there is no fundamental change in how the government views its relationship with West Bank settlers.

Incitement is, according to legal scholars, extraordinarily difficult to prove. It requires stringent and complicated evidentiary standards. In addition, courts are hesitant to rule that speech is incitement as that is the essence of the free speech dilemma. While free speech is the essence of a democracy, protecting the liberty and safety of the innocent is equally important. Not addressing religious extremism invariably and inevitably comes back to "haunt" society and individuals alike. The victims of honor killings are the ultimate manifestation of that acquiescence, if not worse.

Whether in Pakistan, Afghanistan, the Gaza Strip, or Toronto, the fact pattern is chillingly (the word is used deliberately as previously explained) similar. Extremist attitudes lead devout Islamic parents and/or other family members to reach the conclusion that a female family member has violated their family honor. Judge, jury, and executioner are rolled into one as the decision is made to kill her. The justification is a combination of religion and culture. The end is known at the beginning. Perhaps one can argue that the women (in some cases girls) knowingly tempted fate by engaging in conduct they must have or should have known would incur the religious and cultural wrath of family members. Perhaps they could not "help themselves" and were unable or unwilling to refrain from a particular behavior. Perhaps they convinced themselves that harm would not come to them, especially from their own family.

However, at the end of the day, religious and cultural considerations took precedence over the basic parental instinct to protect one's child. In the case before me, the mother's testimony was shocking both with respect to how she described killing her child and the absolute "rightness" (from her perspective) of the act. She had ordered her two sons to kill her daughter and there was no doubt that religion and culture meshed together requiring the act be undertaken. The shame to family honor would have been unbearable had the "shamer" not been killed by her own family. Leaving it to others is to miss the point for the shame was to the family and therefore the killing is to be done by family alone.[4]

Is this religion and culture run amok? Perhaps, but that is to miss its essence. Its essence is that this is the practice of extreme religion/culture that endangers the lives of untold number of young women. Herein lies a fundamental tension between religious liberty and freedom of speech, and the right to life, liberty, and the pursuit of happiness. To kill a young woman because of whom she dates would be considered beyond the pale for non-believers, and even the vast majority of believers. However, it is a requirement for extreme believers or re-articulated, for those who practice extreme religion. Is that a price society is willing to pay for religious liberty and freedom of speech? This is a fundamental question policy makers and the public alike must determine. Re-phrased, the issue can succinctly be stated as follows: "Whose liberty do we primarily protect—the religious extremist or the innocent individual"?

How politics facilitates cultural or religious-based violence is critical to the discussion; after all, if political leadership is unwilling to fully engage lawbreakers for purposes of political expedience then incitement and violence are facilitated. This was brought home to me in a series of conversations with senior civil servants who compellingly argued that the failure of elected officials to proactively condemn rather than tacitly accept violence by religious extremists is critical. The suggestion is not that political leadership is dismissive of religious extremists as is the case with the media, but rather that over-arching political considerations justify a failure to take a hard-headed approach in the face of religious extremism.

The wide range of violent acts that can be committed in the name of religion reflects the extraordinary danger presented when religious-cultural extremism has been culturally institutionalized and accepted as appropriate conduct in an effort to ensure purity, devotion, and protect family honor. In the name of achieving all three, violence, including murder, is not only tolerated, it is accepted as appropriate behavior in the name of protecting religious-cultural extremism. Society clearly pays a

---

4   Although in an honor killing available on YouTube the young woman who was chased by her father was killed by both family and non-family members alike.

price for enabling religious liberty. Cultural considerations when cloaked in religious undertones (or overtones) present an extraordinary threat to society. They also present a clear and present threat to members of a particular religion whose ways conflict with the 'orthodoxy' of that religion. However, as documented in this chapter, that conflict can result in the death of the individual who dares to stand up to cultural realities and considerations. The price for wearing blue jeans and dating the "wrong boy" may well be death. The price for seeking to enforce a legitimate and lawful governmental decision fervently objected to by the lawbreaker who believes that extreme religious and cultural considerations outweigh the law is harm to the law enforcer.

The primary take-away from this litany is that society and individuals alike pay a certain, and sometimes steep, price for tolerating religious and cultural freedom. Conversely, my numerous conversations with respected jurists concerning the possibility of limiting freedom of speech by broadening an incitement definition was generally met with skepticism regarding both the legality and wisdom of doing so. Strong arguments were forcefully presented as to why speech must not be limited and why incitement must be viewed from a limited perspective. While those same distinguished jurists unequivocally understood the dangers inherent to limiting speech they also understood the danger presented by extremist speech.

The speakers and their followers both benefit from the powerful and compelling respect for the law shown by these jurists. The extremist rabbis, priests, and imams take advantage of the tolerance shown by mainstream society with respect to how extremist religion is practiced and manifested. While culture is important, religious based culture must not be a catchword for unpunished violence. Worse than that, it is violence that has been sanctioned by religious authorities with state compliance. The harm does not justify either turning a blind eye nor not considering limiting otherwise protected rights.

CHAPTER NINE

CONFRONTING THE STORM

This book has been unsettling to conceive, research, write, edit, and re-read. I have communicated with hundreds of people from different walks of life, cultures, societies, countries, and viewpoints. The picture painted by these individuals of the danger of religious extremism was most unsettling. What clouds the picture is the unwillingness of many of these same people to support a theory whereby the government would act forcefully against religious extremists. My proposal to address religious extremism, which admittedly requires limiting otherwise guaranteed rights, was largely met with skepticism and concern. That disconnect is particularly troubling for, if we do not address religious extremism, our inaction provides a victory for the extremists.

My only agenda in writing this book was a scholarly pursuit of the truth, and the goal of developing workable recommendations for policy makers. As I have done in previous works, I emphasize putting forth policy recommendations to decision makers. I am a firm proponent of seeking to impact the public debate. Whether addressing the extraordinary failing of the Bush Administration in establishing a torture-based inter-rogation regime in the aftermath of 9/11 to being an early and consistent proponent for establishing "domestic terror courts" in the U.S., to advo-cating cost-benefit and effectiveness-based homeland security strategies, my goal has been simple—to put my professional experience to good use in creating a more legal and effective national security policy.

This book has been different primarily because the subject matter is of such enormous complexity to people of faith and non-believers alike. There may well be no issue more complicated, contentious, and unset-tling than religion. In the classroom I have found it challenging, to say the least, to explain the power of "doing God's work." Perhaps if I were a person of faith it would be easier.

My hope is that this book will provide practical, hopefully adoptable policy recommendations predicated on the rule of law. For people of faith, belief in a Supreme Being is critical to their definition of religion's essence. For people of extreme religious belief, their God is the only God and their Truth is the only Truth. The practical result of that abso-lutism is a de-legitimization of other faiths and others' Gods. That is extraordinarily dangerous. Conversely, when one feels de-legitimized, one will likely respond in kind.

While I have no illusion, pretension, or ambition to 'de-extreme' religious extremism, I believe that society must protect itself more pro-actively and effectively against religious extremism. The fundamental reality of religious extremists is that self-governance, self-imposed restraint, and moderation is beyond their intellectual beliefs. That is not to suggest they are not smart; in fact, quite the opposite. Precisely because they are so "tuned-in" both to their congregants and to the larger society, they have neither the need nor interest to do so. If, as I have come to believe, religious extremists are qualitatively, existentially, and philosophically distinct from other extremists, why should mainstream, secular society expect them to limit their own power? Precisely because their power is predicated on an assumption that their actions are done in the name of their God with the intention and requirement of satisfying that God, restraint in the context of extremism is the manifestation of a lack of faith.

The focus of a religious extremist is single-minded dedication and devotion to serving his God. Based on innumerable conversations with terrorists and members of the intelligence community alike I have written elsewhere of the extraordinary hardships imposed on wanted terrorists. I have come to the conclusion that those hardships, when understood in the context of the terrorists serving their God, are both "explainable" and "tolerable." While difficult, these hardships are not nearly as foreboding as the alternative, according to their worldview, as they believe it. For them it is better to incur physical discomfort than to incur the wrath of God.

Where does that leave the secular state? Precisely because of the absolutism of the religious extremist, I recommend that the state has no choice but to respond accordingly. Perhaps the fundamental weakness of my argument is that I am suggesting that the state restrict the rights of citizens. In presenting this thesis to different forums including academic, religious, and policy makers in the countries surveyed, I am generally met with concern, if not outright opposition, regarding the essence of my proposal. However, I believe society may have no choice but to consider some of the measures listed in this book. It clearly has no choice but to discuss these and other similar proposals.

I have consistently reminded the reader that there is no hidden agenda behind this book; I have no intention in engaging in religion bashing.

I will leave that unnecessary, uninteresting, and rather futile effort to others. What I do suggest is that people of faith must work in close cooperation with non-believers and decision makers to address the danger presented by religious extremists. I am an advocate of what is referred to as the multiple audience theory, meaning that dilemmas and paradigms must be viewed from the perspective of particular audiences. While akin to the Rashomon effect,[1] my suggestion is different because it does not emphasize how two people view the same issue differently but suggests that each dilemma is understood and conceptualized differently by different interest groups. That said, I would advocate that these three different groups—religious moderates, non-believers, and government—have a common interest. That common interest is preserving our rights, liberties, and protections, as we know them today.

This suggested coalition must come to grips with the idea that religious extremism presents a danger to contemporary society. Maybe not in all societies, or to all members of all societies, but to enough segments of society that specific measures must be weighed and considered, starting with the most general and working towards more specific solutions depending on the unique situations.

I have suggested in previous chapters that the *Brandenburg* test of "imminent" danger in the speech context clearly favors the skillful speaker able to address his audience without directly inciting them to action. Without sounding cynical or facetious, the image of Alfred E. Newman's famous "What Me" cartoon of the boy with a sly grin is an appropriate visual suggestion. The fire in the theatre test has been met; there is, by analogy, fire in the theatre today. Forced marriage and sexual relations involving 14-year-old girls, honor killings of Islamic women believed to have violated "modesty" standards, and what the Prime Minister of Israel termed pogroms[2] in describing the actions of religious extremists in the West Bank with respect to their unconscionable and criminal conduct directed at Palestinians and IDF soldiers and policemen are the fire.

That fire has been set, stoked, and fueled by extreme religious leaders. The power of the pastor, rabbi, and imam is different than that of any secular leader today. While previous secular leaders such as Hitler,

---

1   The Rashomon Effect in anthropology is used to describe how the observers filter what is observed through their own experiences.

2   The term pogrom refers to large-scale, targeted, and repeated anti-Semitic violence.

Stalin, Mao, and Pol Pot have led their followers to do brutal and unimaginable acts, the present threat is different. Today's greatest threat is violent religious extremists. The state must act now to prevent them from becoming the monsters of tomorrow. I propose that limiting certain aspects of the exercise of religion may be the only way to do so.

The freedom to exercise religion involves two primary rights—the right to free speech and the right to exercise religion. My recommendation of expanding *Brandenburg* is problematic both constitutionally and politically. Even so, I believe that limiting speech if it is anticipatorily deemed to present a threat to public order is necessary at times. This test will be relevant to all speech, including religious speech. While admittedly my primary concern is with respect to religious speech, I am not specifically targeting religious speech. Because of my profound concern with respect to religious speech, I recommend that religious speech be subject to the same careful scrutiny as secular speech. If that means that intelligence and security agencies will attend religious services with pen and paper in hand just as secular speech is observed, then so be it. There can be no more immunity granted to priests, rabbis, and imams. When congregants believe these leaders speak directly to God, and for him, their power to influence the actions of their members can become dangerous. This danger cannot go unchecked.

The concerned voice will ask, "how anticipatory is anticipatory?" I suggest framing the discussion in a self-defense paradigm. The Caroline Doctrine in customary international law articulates an "imminent attack" test for determining when a state can act to prevent an attack on its soil. In the aftermath of World War II, Article 51 of the United Nations Charter deliberately sought to limit self-defense to those circumstances only in the aftermath of armed attack. I suggest that the present danger posed by religious clerics requires re-articulating *when* otherwise protected speech must be restricted.

When is anticipatory? That answer requires a contextual analysis that examines the following four criteria: the speaker, the audience, the past acts and conduct of the speaker, and the acts that have been committed in the aftermath of his speech in the past. That four-part test will not be liberally applied. Rather the test will be broadly and strictly applied simultaneously. Broadly as in an expansive view of incitement, strictly as in not tolerating speech that has historically gone unpunished.

Does this test raise legitimate concerns amongst those who jealously protect First Amendment rights? It should and must. However, there is an additional audience at play who is *no less* deserving of state protection. That audience includes otherwise unprotected individuals and groups who are, to a certain extent, the victims of free speech protections.

On December 8, 2008, I met with the Justice Minister of the Government of Holland, Dr. Hirsch Ballin. He was extraordinarily gracious both with his time and his patience in answering my questions. During the course of our conversation, Minister Ballin told me of proposed legislation before the Dutch parliament that would limit speech deemed blasphemous or offensive if it were deemed not to have public utility or purpose. I took that as a legislative effort to prevent a repeat of the publication of the cartoon drawing of the prophet Muhammad originally published in a Danish newspaper. While Minister Ballin couched the impetus for the legislation in the context of meeting various European legislative requirements regarding hate speech and civil rights I found myself asking the following question, "What about restricting the free speech right of extreme imams who are engaging in the radicalization of Moroccan youth?"

Theo van Gogh's killer, Mohammed Bouyeri, was not incited to murder in a vacuum. Perhaps Van Gogh was provocative, even offensive. However, under no circumstance is that a crime and under no condition can it justify murder. Bouyeri was a member of the Hofstad group, which was infused with religious-based hatred by a religious extremist leader whose words led to a terrible crime. In the context of who and what are we protecting, did Van Gogh not deserve protection? Of course he did. My concern is that many decision makers are too hesitant to enact proper legislation for fear of offending these particular extremist groups.

Whether the reason is "political correctness" or genuine fear of "offending" is irrelevant. What I suggest is that the price borne by society as a whole due to religious extremist speech is intolerable. Critics of this proposal have responded that isolated attacks are not justification for limiting otherwise guaranteed protections. I understand the significance of recommending the imposition of limits on freedoms, so it is with great trepidation that I respectfully disagree and recommend limiting free speech. The means would be expanding *Brandenburg*. In the Israeli context, it means applying the fundamental point made by former Justice Zamir—practically applying lessons learned from Rabin's assassination. My candid and generous meetings with senior Israeli leaders suggested that the approach to investigating and prosecuting right-wing extremist rabbis is "why," rather than "why not."

On the very days that the Israeli media reports that extremist settlers are openly challenging the state and acting on the words of specific individuals, the "why" approach is dangerous to democracy, not the "why not." Only asking "why" facilitates the danger that extremist religious leaders pose to Israeli democracy. While political realities are enormously complicated in Israel there is another option—examining speech with an eye towards prosecution rather than with the current approach that can, at best, be defined as circumspect.

Some of the issues discussed in this book are not legal but rather raise important questions regarding the policy of tolerance. The title of Martha Minow's article, "Tolerance in an Age of Terror," best articulates the dilemma facing democracies. The French and Turks have addressed the issue concisely and directly by banning headscarves. Why? In the French paradigm it is because the state is 'above all' and any imposition on that ethos is viewed negatively. It is unclear if the French rationale for the banning is predicated on a threat-based analysis or rather because of how the French view the relationship between the state and other entities. Be that as it may, the end result is a manifestation that the state should be placed before other entities.

In the Turkish paradigm, the rationale is more complicated. For a secular democracy confronted by an increasingly religious core the scarf represents anti-modernity. Needless to say, the tension in Turkey with respect to religious and secular Islam is enormously complicated when the leading political party is, in essence, religious. While the European Court of Justice has upheld the Turkish decision to ban the scarf, I would suggest this is not a legal issue. It is, rather, one of policy; the policy of the limits of the exercise of religion. Whether the scarf is a religious or cultural symbol is a matter of debate. Perhaps it is one of those "depends who you ask" paradigms. What is critical is that the scarf, whether religious or cultural, has been banned. What is interesting is that Turkey is a country that is on the cusp of secularism, yet has strong religious roots, is modern, yet not Western and has decided that the scarf is the symbol of this enormously complicated internal "conflict."

In so deciding, the Turkish government has limited the free exercise of religion (on the premise that the scarf wearer does so for religious purposes). While different from the French rationale, the result is the same. Does this reflect a perception that the scarf represents a "threat" to

Turkish society? In the context of the proposed actual-perceived threat analysis it is unclear in which category the Turkish government assigns the scarf. There is a different question that is appropriate to ask but whose analysis is beyond our purview—does banning the scarf minimize religious faith and belief? Because the answer is all but certainly "no," the question (from a practical-policy perspective) is, why would the Turkish government ban the scarf?

Policy considerations must be weighed from a cost-benefit perspective reflecting prioritization, risk, and threat assessment. To that end, while the policy is conceivably understandable in the context of Turkey's tenuous democracy and concern with an increasing "Islamization" (that is, newly revived religiosity in a population of 99 percent Muslims), the over-riding consideration must be strategic rather than tactical. It is unclear if at the end of the day the Turkish government's policy, validated by the courts, will genuinely contribute to minimizing religious extremism in a nation of extraordinary geo-political significance to the West.

As concerned as the French and Turks have been with respect to the scarf, the Netherlands have taken different tacks. In my conversation with Justice Minister Ballin, he suggested that while the Netherlands has a long history of tolerance, it also has a history of persecuting religious minorities. In the same vein, while the Netherlands is a country of historical immigration (Jews, Turks, Surinamese, Alites, and Moroccans) it has recently implemented restrictions on immigration. The tension is critical for it reflects openness mixed with caution, tolerance mixed with intolerance. Perhaps this "yin and yang" manifests itself in banning the *burkha* while not banning the scarf.

When I suggested to the Justice Minister that perhaps the Netherlands is at the focus of the question of where Europe as a whole will go, he was surprised; I explained that if viewed from a spectrum analysis, one can suggest that Turkey and France are at one extreme and England at the other with the Netherlands in the middle. To that end, he suggested that the Netherlands would not ban the scarf, as that would be too reflective of intolerance. Perhaps. Time and events will tell.

On the other hand, cultural-religious relativism cannot and must not tolerate murder in the name of religion. Honor killing is a euphemism for a brutal murder of an unprotected female either by family or community. There is no honor in the act. There is no honor in suggesting that the individual killed was merely another victim of domestic violence. That is worse than disingenuous. Society must protect the vulnerable and otherwise unprotected. To that end, religious extremists, however they couch their language, calling on male family members to protect family honor must be limited in their free speech. This is the essence of the contextual argument, for speaker and audience understand each other implicitly and there is no need for a direct order. That is the fundamental weakness of the *Brandenburg* test and exemplifies exactly why religious extremist speech must be limited.

Where does all this leave us?

Answering that question takes me back to the dedication page of this book. By analogy, if Anne Frank represents eternal optimism in the face of the unimaginable, and Sandra Samuel is the manifestation of extraordinary courage by an ordinary human being facing down murderous killers, then the nation states discussed in this book represent timidity in facing religious extremism.

I am careful, even extremely cautious in distinguishing between religion and religious extremism. The former represents the good in society; the latter endangers non-believers, as well as people of moderate faith and government. Religious extremists, particularly their faith leaders, do not represent a perceived threat, they represent an actual threat. Criminal law allows the individual to act in self-defense when threatened; international law enables the state to act in self-defense when threatened.

That threat analysis leads me to the problematic and troubling conclusion that the state must apply self-defense measures in the face of religious extremism. We cannot allow ourselves to justify actions of religious extremist by articulating contextualism. My interlocutor in the Dutch intelligence service who suggested I understand the "context" of the *fatwa* that Darwish issued against Marcouch disturbingly misses the imminent danger. The text, whether verbal or written, must be understood from the perspective of the audience, not from how the intelligence officer views it or believes the intended audience views it. The *fatwa* was not intended for the intelligence community. Darwish knows his audience and tailors his message to them.

When I had dinner with Marcouch he understood the threat. He knew that Darwish had an audience and that the audience understands what it is told. The message was clear to Marcouch, after all he was the potential target. Pretending it does not exist will not erase the actual threat. The reality must be looked squarely in the eye precisely as Sandra Samuel looked evil in the eye. She understood the threat and acted.

A two-year-old child owes his life to her courage in the face of an impending violent death. While Anne Frank has passed on, her voice rings loud 60 years later. I believe she understood the fate that awaited her.

This book is intended to act as a clarion call to action. Action defined as legislation which rearticulates the limits of free speech. Action defined as political courage both in the face of religious violence facing inward that only harms members of the faith as well as the moral courage to truly determine what presents a threat to the state. What is determined to be a threat must be limited, while allowing harmless practices to go unencumbered. While I clearly call for limiting certain rights, I am equally suspicious of executive excess. Precisely for that reason I remain skeptical as to the wisdom of banning the scarf while I understand the security considerations in banning the *burkha*.

At the end of the day, the decision to limit or ban must be predicated on what I define as criteria-based, rational decision-making. The tension or balance between threats and rights must be carefully weighed. Denying the danger is dangerous; granting limitless immunity to extremist inciters is to knowingly endanger the unprotected. Justice Jackson's words ring true today, "the Constitution is not a suicide pact." Victims of religious extremism deserve our protection. Limiting the right of rabbis, priests, and imams who incite in whatever fashion, is the first step to minimizing the number of future victims. This is society's primary obligation. Wishing it was not so is a mistake of historic proportions. Engaging in excess is also a mistake of historic proportions. Understanding the threat is the critical first step. After that, the state must act where there is a threat and not act where one does not exist. That is the essence of lawful, proactive civil democracies.

The time to act is now.

RECOMMENDED READING LIST

Appiah, Kwame Anthony, *Cosmopolitanism* (W.W. Norton, 2007).

Armstrong, Karen, *The Battle for God* (Random House, 2000).

– A cogent and thoughtful analysis of fundamentalism and extremism.

Asad, Talal, *Formations of the Secular* (Stanford University Press, 2003).

– An important analysis of the relationship between secularism and religion.

Atran, Scott, *In Gods We Trust* (Oxford University Press, 2002).

– An important examination of religion from an anthropological perspective.

Bagley, Will, *Blood of the Prophets* (University of Oklahoma Press, Norman Publishing, 2002).

– Critical reading for understanding the Mountain Meadows Massacre.

Bawer, Bruce, *While Europe Slept* (Broadway Books, 2006).

– A provocative analysis about Islam and/in Europe.

Boyer, Pascal, *Religion Explained* (Basic Books, 2001).

– An important book in seeking to understand the power of religion.

Brandon, James & Hafez, Salam, *Crimes of the Community: Honour-based violence in the UK* (The Centre for Social Cohesion, 2008).

Bromley, David G. & Melton, J. Gordon eds., *Cults, Religion & Violence* (Cambridge University Press, 2002).

Brooks, Juanita, *The Mountain Meadows Massacre* (University of Oklahoma Press, Norman Publishing, 1991).

– Critical/path-breaking analysis of the Mountain Meadows Massacre.

Brugger, Herausgegeben von Winfried & Karayanni, Michael, *Religion in the Public Sphere: A Comparative Analysis of German, Israeli, American and International Law* (Springer-Verlag, 2007).

Burleigh, Michael, *Sacred Causes* (Harper Perennial, 2008).

- An important analysis of religion and politics.

Dawkins, Richard, *The God Delusion* (Houghton Mifflin, 2008).

Dayan, Joan, *Haiti, History, and the Gods* (University of California Press, 1995).

- Thoughtful examination of culture.

Dennett, Daniel C., *Breaking the Spell* (Penguin Group, 2007).

Deseret Book Company, *The Doctrine and Covenants* (Deseret Book Company, 1961).

Eisgruber, Christopher L. & Sager, Lawrence G., *Religious Freedom and the Constitution* (Harvard University Press, 2007).

- Critical for understanding the relationship between religious freedom and the Constitution.

Firmage, Edwin Brown & Mangrum, Richard Collin, *Zion in the Courts* (University of Illinois Press, 2001) (1988).

- Critical analysis of the relationship between the Mormon Church, religious liberty, and protection of religious minorities.

Fradkin, Hillel, & Haqqani, Husain & Brown, Eric eds., *Current Trends in Islamist Ideology* (Hudson Institute, Vol. 6 2008).

Gen. Intelligence & Security Serv., *The Radical Dawa in Transition* (2007).

Gibb, Sir Hamilton A.R., *Mohammedanism* (New American Library, 1955).

- Important survey of Islam.

Griffith, Lee, *The War on Terrorism and the Terror of God* (Wm. B. Eerdmans Publishing Co., 2002).

- Thoughtful analysis of religious violence.

Harris, Lee, *The Suicide of Reason* (Basic Books, 2007).

Harris, Sam, *The End of Faith* (The Free Press, 2006).

- Raises important questions regarding religion and reason.

Haynes, Jeffrey ed., *The Politics of Religion* (Routledge, 2006).

FREEDOM FROM RELIGION

HM Government, *The Prevent Strategy: A Guide for Local Partners in England* (2008).

Hobbes, Thomas, *Leviathan* (Michael Oakeshott ed., Macmillan Publishing Co., 1975).

- The classic on political philosophy; critical for understand religious authority.

Ibrahim, Raymond ed., *The Al Qaeda Reader* (Broadway Books, 2007).

Joseph Smith's "New Translation" of the Bible (Herald Publishing House, 1970).

Karsh, Efraim, *Islamic Imperialism* (Yale University Press, 2006).

Kimball, Charles, *When Religion Becomes Evil* (HarperSanFrancisco, 2003).

- Important for understanding the difference between religion and religious extremism.

Krakauer, Jon, *Under the Banner of Heaven* (Anchor Books, 2004).

- Essential for understanding the Mormon faith.

Larsson, J.P., *Understanding Religious Violence* (Ashgate Publishing, 2004).

- Essential for understanding relationship between religion and violence.

Lewis, Anthony, *Freedom for the Thought That We Hate* (Basic Books, 2007).

- Essential for understanding the First Amendment.

Lewis, Bernard, *The Crisis of Islam* (Random House Trade Paperbacks, 2004).

- Essential in seeking to understand contemporary Islam.

Lewis, Bernard, *What Went Wrong?* (Harper Perennial, 2003).

- Essential in seeking to understand contemporary Islam.

MacEoin, Denis, *The Hijacking of British Islam* (Policy Exchange, 2007).

Marshall, Paul A. ed., *Religious Freedom in the World* (Rowman & Littlefield Publishers, Inc., 2008).

McConnell, Michael W., *The Origins and Historical Understanding of Free Exercise of Religion*, 103 HARV. L. REV. 1409 n.7 (1990).

- A seminal law review article examining the free exercise of religion.

Meacham, Jon, *American Gospel* (Random House, 2006).

- An invaluable analysis of religion and politics.

Michael, George, *The Enemy of My Enemy* (University Press of Kansas, 2006).

Murray, Douglas & Verwey, Johan Pieter, *Victims of Intimidation* (The Centre for Social Cohesion, 2008).

Razack, Sherene H., *Casting Out: the Eviction of Muslims from Western Law & Politics* (University of Toronto Press Inc., 2008).

Seiple, Robert A. & Hoover, Dennis R., eds., *Religion & Security* (Rowman & Littlefield Publishers, Inc., 2004).

Sheleg, Yair, *The Political and Social Ramifications of Evacuating Settlements in Judea, Samaria, and the Gaza Strip* (Policy Paper 72, The Israel Democracy Institute 2007) (Hebrew).

- Essential for understanding disengagement from the West Bank and the Gaza Strip.

Shetreet, Shimon, *Between Three Branches of Government* (Floersheimer Institute for Policy Studies, 2001).

- Essential in understanding the relationship between religious and civil rights in Israel.

Smith, Christian, *American Evangelicalism* (University of Chicago Press, 1998).

- Critical in understanding American Evangelicalism.

Smith, Jonathan Z., *Imagining Religion* (University of Chicago Press, 1982).

Stark, Rodney & Finke, Roger, *Acts of Faith* (Universiry of California Press, 2000).

Stern, Jessica, *Terror in the Name of God* (HarperCollins, 2003).

- Important for understanding the motivations of terrorists.

Sullivan, Winnifred Fallers, *The Impossibility of Religious Freedom* (Princeton University Press 2005).

- Important book for understanding religious freedom and the law.

Waldman, Steve, *Founding Faith* (Random House, 2008).

- Essential for understanding religious freedom in the context of American history.

Walker, Ronald W. & Turley Jr., Richard E. & Leonard, Glen M., *Massacre at Mountain Meadows* (Oxford University Press, 2008).

- Important, current analysis of the Mountain Meadows Massacre.

Weinberg, Leonard & Pedahzur, Ami eds., *Religious Fundamentalism and Political Extremism* (Frank Cass Publishers, 2004).

Wilson, David Sloan, *Darwin's Cathedral* (University of Chicago Press 2002).

Wright, Robin, *Sacred Rage* (Touchstone, 2001).

- Important analysis of Islamic extremism.

Ye'Or, Bat, *Eurabia: The Euro-Arab Axis* (Farleigh Dickinson University Press, 2007).

Zertal, Idith & Eldar, Akiva, *Lords of the Land* (Nation Books, 2007).

- Must read for understanding relationship between Israeli politicians and Jewish settlements in the West Bank.

APPENDIX

Understanding Constitutional Review: A Cheat Sheet

by RuthAnne Frost

Prophets and Polygamy: The Fundamentalist Church of Jesus Christ of Latter-Day Saints

by Brady G. Stuart

The Secular-Religious Divide in Turkey

by Artemis Vamianakis

UNDERSTANDING CONSTITUTIONAL REVIEW: A CHEAT SHEET

RuthAnne Frost[†]

STANDARD OF REVIEW

The concept of "standard of review" is discussed so much in law school that lawyers often consider it common knowledge. Understanding standard of review is key to understanding constitutional law itself. From a layman's perspective, the idea is relatively simple and involves three questions. First, one must ask, *"What is the liberty interest at stake?"* This liberty interest can be the freedom of privacy, right to be free from racial or gender discrimination, right to speak, right to practice religion, right to due process, right to own a weapon, etc.

This question is of paramount importance, for sometimes the lawyer who describes the liberty interest in the more compelling way is the lawyer who wins the case. For example, consider *Bowers v. Hardwick*, 478 U.S. 186 (1986), where Justice White wrote that the question before the court was whether the Constitution creates "a fundamental right upon homosexuals to engage in sodomy." Then consider *Lawrence v. Texas*, which overruled *Bowers*, and said that the liberty interest in question was "intimate, adult consensual conduct" taking place in the private realm. 539 U.S. 558 (2003).

The second question one must ask is, *"What is the appropriate level of scrutiny for this liberty interest?"* Fundamental liberties are the most safeguarded in our society—speech, religion, the right to be free of racial discrimination, etc. Judges and lawyers often disagree about what is and is not fundamental, but all agree that fundamental liberties are entitled to the greatest protections. This protection is known as "strict scrutiny."

Intermediate liberties are those which are important, but not quite as protected as fundamental liberties. As the name implies, these liberties receive "intermediate scrutiny." It can often be very difficult to separate

---

[†]   J.D. Candidate May 2009, S.J. Quinney College of Law, University of Utah. I'd like to thank Professor Amos Guiora for the opportunity to write this article and work on this book.

intermediate liberties from fundamental liberties, as well as from the lower types of liberty interests that receive the least protection. For example, the Supreme Court of the United States has held that the right to be free of racial discrimination is a fundamental liberty interest. This is because racial minorities are potentially subject to stereotyping; they have suffered a history of discrimination; the physical characteristics that separate one race from another are immutable; their group is "discrete," meaning racial minorities are easily recognizable; and their group is "insular," meaning they are easily excluded from the political and social life of the majority. See *Korematsu v. United States*, 323 U.S. 214 (1944). Furthermore, the historical intent of the post-Civil War amendments (outlawing slavery, making African-Americans citizens and protecting them from state governments that would deprive them of their liberties, and ensuring their right to vote) was to protect racial minorities from discrimination. For these reasons, classifications based on race are highly suspect.

Classifications based on gender, however, are only subject to intermediate scrutiny. This may seem a bit illogical at first—after all, are women not also subject to the dangers of stereotyping and a history of discrimination? Is gender not immutable, just as race is? While these things are true, gender is slightly different than race for two important reasons. First, while a gender group is "discrete" in that anyone can tell whether you are a man or woman, gender groups are not insular. Excluding men or women from the social or political life of the majority is not possible, given that men and women each form half the population. Second, while the right of women to vote is guaranteed by the Nineteenth Amendment, the Constitution does not specifically spell out protections based on gender classifications in a manner similar to the Civil War amendments. This second point is admittedly debatable—the Fourteenth Amendment, after all, has been extended to groups other than African-Americans, including women.

The remaining liberties are considered "low value," and include economic liberties. These liberties are entitled to what is called "rational basis" scrutiny. Low value liberties include what might be termed "economic liberties." For example, in *United States Railroad Retirement Board v. Fritz*, 449 U.S. 166 (1980), the Supreme Court examined a retirement benefits plan that resulted in some employees getting dual benefits. The fact that the legislation was economic in nature triggered the rational basis standard of review for judicial assessment of that plan.

The third question one must ask is, *"Does the government action meet the level of scrutiny?"* To answer this question, we must determine two things. First, what is the government's interest? And second, how has the government sought to address this interest?

If the liberty interest has been deemed fundamental, entitling it to strict scrutiny, the government has the burden of showing that its interest is compelling, and that it has created the most narrowly tailored remedy to address this problem. Narrow tailoring requires that the government action be neither over- nor under-inclusive. An over-inclusive regulation encompasses too much; an under-inclusive regulation fails to address essential parts of the compelling interest. Generally, this requires that the government use the least restrictive means available for achieving its interests.

Speech is generally considered a fundamental liberty. When the government seeks to restrict the content of speech, it is required to meet the requirements of strict scrutiny. See *Reno v. ACLU*, 521 U.S. 844 (1997), striking down indecency provisions of the Communications Decency Act. For example, in *Cohen v. California*, 403 U.S. 15 (1971), the Supreme Court held that a state cannot bar the use of offensive words (in this case, a jacket that read "Fuck the Draft" on the back) simply because such words are likely to cause a violent reaction in the audience, or because the state wishes to protect public morality.

If the liberty interest is intermediate, the government must show that its regulation involves an important governmental interest that is furthered by substantially related means. See *Craig v. Boren*, which struck down an Oklahoma statute that created different drinking ages for men and women. Note that this standard is relaxed from strict scrutiny, making it easier for the government to meet its burden.

If the liberty interest is low value, then rational basis is applied. Under rational basis, the government action is almost always upheld. So long as the government asserts a legitimate purpose and the law or regulation in question bears a reasonable relationship to that purpose, courts will uphold the law as constitutional. Unlike in strict scrutiny, where "fit" questions are paramount, under rational basis the government is allowed to achieve its purposes "one step at a time." For example, *Railway Express Agency v. New York*, 335 U.S. 106 (1949) held that a traffic regulation forbidding advertising on street vehicles was Constitutional. The Court noted that, given a rational basis review, the function of the court "is not to weigh evidence on . . . whether the regulation is sound or appropriate, nor to pass judgment on the wisdom of the regulation," which the government asserted was to promote traffic safety.

Under the rational basis test, questions of over- and under-inclusiveness are similarly irrelevant. For example, the Supreme Court has upheld a regulation that prevents those in methadone programs from holding Transit Authority positions, even though it was over-inclusive in that it excluded methadone users who presented no safety risk, and under-inclusive in that it did not address the safety issues that non-methadone users could still pose. *New York City Transit Authority v. Beazer*, 440 U.S. 568 (1979). This case also shows us that the government may assert cost-effectiveness in presenting its case. New York could have evaluated each case involving a methadone user individually, but it would have been expensive to do so. Under rational basis, a regulation will not be struck down simply because a better, but more expensive, alternative is available.

This does not mean, however, that the government will always prevail at the rational basis level. In *City of Cleburne v. Cleburne Living Center*, for example, the Supreme Court held that laws impacting the mentally retarded are not to be given heightened scrutiny, but a zoning ordinance that forbade the construction of a group home represented an "irrational prejudice against the mentally retarded." The Court ruled against the government. See 473 U.S. 432 (1985).

After determining the answers to these three questions—what is the liberty interest, what is the appropriate level of scrutiny, and does the government action meet the applicable test—a Court will hold whether or not a law or regulation is Constitutional.

PROPHETS AND POLYGAMY: THE FUNDAMENTALIST CHURCH OF JESUS CHRIST OF LATTER-DAY SAINTS

Brady G. Stuart[†]

Recently, the Fundamentalist Church of Jesus Christ of Latter-Day Saints (FLDS) has been the focus of intense government and media scrutiny because of their practice of plural marriage involving underage girls. Many of these girls are as young as 14 when their prophet proclaims that God has commanded them to marry men as much as three times their age. These girls, and their parents, submit to the outrageous demand because they believe that the words of their prophet are in fact the words of God.

This paper will focus on three areas to help the reader better understand the danger that the FLDS leadership poses to specific members of their own group. The first area is the history of the original LDS church, from which the FLDS church is an offshoot, including their belief in divine revelation from prophets and plural marriage. The second is the government intervention that has taken place regarding both the leadership of the church and their members. The third is the isolation the FLDS church has fostered, and how the limited contact has affected members' perceptions of the outside world.

HISTORY OF THE CHURCH OF JESUS CHRIST OF LATTER-DAY SAINTS

The history of the FLDS church begins with the foundation of the original Church of Jesus Christ of Latter-Day Saints, often referred to as the Mormon Church, by Joseph Smith. In the spring of 1820, Joseph Smith, a boy of 14, struggled to decide which church he should join in his small New York town. He decided to pray and ask God which church was true. Smith said that as an answer to his prayer he was visited by God the Father, and his son, Jesus Christ. They told Joseph that none of the churches were true, and that he would help restore the true church once again. Through subsequent revelations and visions, Joseph Smith said he was ordained as a prophet of God, and given additional scriptures, including accounts from ancient prophets on the American continent, known as the Book of Mormon.

[†]   Juris Doctor 2009, University of Utah. It has been my privilege to be one of Amos Guiora's research assistants for this book.

These miraculous claims led Joseph Smith's followers to believe he had a divine connection with God and was his spokesman and prophet on the earth. Unquestioning obedience to the latter-day prophet was regularly taught to church members. They believed that the only way to heaven was to follow the commandments of the prophet. This faith was so strong that members were willing to do almost anything for Smith. This faith was tested in the 1830s as Smith gradually began introducing polygamy to the members of his church, claiming that it was a divinely inspired practice.

However, it wasn't until 1852, eight years after Smith's death, that the church officially acknowledged the practice of polygamy under the leadership of their new prophet, Brigham Young. Young was also the prophet that led the Mormons across the continent to settle in Utah in order to escape the intense persecution members faced for their unique religious beliefs.

As members of the church began to congregate in Utah, polygamy became a part of their culture as well as their religion. Utah's population increased dramatically as the church sent missionaries around the world to preach their new gospel. New converts were called to Utah, where they were taught they would establish the new Zion. Utah quickly developed into a unique frontier theocracy under Brigham Young's guidance.

As Utah developed, church leaders saw the benefit of becoming a state. However, the United States strongly opposed polygamy and refused to grant statehood while it was practiced. Outside pressure to stop polygamy increased as the church grew in Utah. In 1856, the newly created Republican party declared that, "It is the duty of Congress to prohibit in the territories those twin relics of barbarism, polygamy and slavery." True to its promise, the Republican party sent federal law enforcement to Utah to do everything they could to end polygamy, including arresting men who practiced it and confiscating their land and possessions.

After years of outside opposition to polygamy, the church finally rescinded the practice. On October 6, 1890, the church's then prophet, Wilford Woodruff, released an official declaration stating that they would obey the laws of the federal government and cease polygamy. Woodruff explained to the members of the church that he had spoken with God, and that he had been shown a vision in which the church would be destroyed if they continued practicing polygamy. Most of the members followed the new commandment from Woodruff, but some believed that he was a fallen prophet who had succumbed to pressure from the United States.

FUNDAMENTALIST OFFSHOOT

Some of those that refused to give up polygamy, believing it was an eternal principle, were the predecessors of the Fundamentalist Church of Jesus Christ of Latter-Day Saints. FLDS members claim that in 1886, four years before the church's renunciation of polygamy, the then prophet and president of the church, John Taylor received a very different revelation. According to FLDS historians, in Taylor's revelation the Lord declared that polygamy was an everlasting covenant, and that he would never revoke it. Lorin C. Woolley, who later became a leader in the FLDS church, testified that he was outside Taylor's room during this vision when he saw a light appearing from beneath the door. Woolley claims to have heard three distinct voices coming from the room, which Taylor later told him was the Lord and the deceased prophet Joseph Smith, who had come to deliver the revelation of eternal polygamy. FLDS members claim that the following morning Taylor placed five men under covenant to practice polygamy as long as they lived, and gave them power to ordain others to do the same.

For some time, this offshoot polygamist group stayed in Salt Lake City, alongside the original Mormon culture. However, as polygamy became less acceptable in mainstream Utah, many of the polygamists went into hiding. Eventually Short Creek, Arizona (now known as Colorado City), became a strong-hold for polygamists. FLDS members felt comfortable in this remote area. Surrounded by desert and over 100 miles away from law enforcement, they believed they could safely practice polygamy unbothered by the outside world.

GOVERNMENT INTERVENTION

The FLDS belief that they would not be bothered by law enforcement for their polygamist practices was mistaken. There have been several raids by government officials on FLDS compounds that have dramatically affected the view and opinion of church members regarding the outside world. One of the most traumatic raids for the FLDS members is known as the Short Creek Raid.

In the summer of 1953, over a hundred Arizona police officers and National Guardsmen descended on the FLDS compound in Short Creek.

The reason given for the raid by Arizona Governor John Pyle, was to stop a pending insurrection by the polygamists. He accused FLDS members of being involved in the "foulest conspiracy you could possibly imagine" that was designed to produce white slaves. The governor even invited reporters to come witness the raid with him.

However, the attempt to demonize those practicing polygamy failed. Church members had been tipped off to the impending raid. As law enforcement entered the compound they found all the adults in the community congregated in a schoolhouse singing hymns, while their children played outside. Instead of reporting on the evils of polygamy, the media focused on the overreaction of government officials. Regardless of media reaction, the government still removed over 236 children from their families at Short Creek. For more than 150 of those children, it took over two years to be reunited with their families.

Beginning in 2004, the government began to pursue the FLDS church once again. This time government officials went after the current prophet, Warren Jeffs, directly. In 2004, several of Jeffs nephews alleged to have been sodomized by Jeffs and his brothers in the late 1980s, leading to a lawsuit against Jeffs and his brothers. Things continued to worsen for the prophet. In 2005, Jeffs was charged with sexual assault on a minor and with conspiracy to commit sexual misconduct with a minor for arranging a marriage between a 14-year-old girl and her 19-year-old first cousin. In late 2005, Jeffs was placed on the FBI's most wanted list, and featured on the television show America's Most Wanted. Jeffs was wanted on charges in both Utah and Arizona. As a fugitive, Jeffs still continued to perform marriages between underage girls and older men.

On August 28, 2006, Jeffs was pulled over for a routine traffic stop and was arrested. His car contained four computers, 16 cell phones, several disguises, and more than $55,000 in cash. Jeffs was sentenced to 10 years in prison. It is believed that Jeffs is still leading the church from prison. Although he has given up his title as president of the church, he still retains the mantle of prophet.

The FLDS church faced more problems at one of their compounds, the Yearning for Zion Ranch, near Eldorado, Texas. On April 16, 2008, Texas state authorities entered the community after they had received several hoax calls impersonating an abused child from the ranch. Child Protective Services determined that the children needed to be protected from the forced underage marriages. This time 416 children were removed from the FLDS compound. Over 100 adult women also chose to leave the ranch in order to accompany their children. The state determined that of the 53 girls aged 14–17, 31 have children or are pregnant. On May 22, 2008, the court ruled that there was not enough evidence to justify keeping the children in state custody. The children were returned to their families within 10 days.

FLDS PERCEPTION OF OUTSIDE WORLD

The Short Creek Raid became a rallying cry for FLDS members, as a manifestation of the wicked secular world's desire to destroy God's chosen people. The memory of losing their children further segregated members from the outside world. This segregation was dramatically increased by the orders of the prophet Warren Jeffs.

The segregation from the secular world and the almighty power that a latter-day prophet possessed was again solidified when Warren Jeffs came to power after the death of Rulon Jeffs, his father, in 2002. Warren Jeffs used his prophetic mantle to deem many of his actions as sanctioned by God. Shortly after his father's death, Jeffs married all but two of his fathers 20 wives, bringing his total number of wives to around 70 according to some ex-members. Jeffs claimed that this was to ensure the preservation of his sacred bloodline. As the only person who possessed the authority to perform marriages, and assign wives, Jeffs often used this power to discipline members by reassigning their wives, children, and homes to another man. This was demonstrated in 2004 when Jeffs exiled 20 male members from the community and assigned their wives to more worthy men. Like his predecessors, Jeffs teaches that it is only through plural marriage that a man may enter heaven. He has taught that any worthy male member should have at least three wives, and the more wives one has, the closer he is to heaven. This practice has led to frequent reports of young male members being thrown out of the community due to their alleged competition with the elder more established members for women.

This power is not only spiritual, it is also monetary. The FLDS church owns the vast majority of all the real estate and property where the members live. Members who want to remain with their families in the community have no choice but to obey every word of their prophet. Until recently, the land owned by the church was estimated to be worth over $100 million. For most FLDS members, the pressure of losing their heavenly blessing as well as their entire temporal well-being forces them to obey every word Jeffs utters.

Jeffs further increased the isolation of his members when he told them to remove their children from public schools. Attendance in the school district, which had 1200 students, immediately dropped to only 250. Jeffs ordered the students to be home schooled, where their curriculum consisted of recorded lectures by Jeffs regarding religion and his view of the world, rather than normal topics such as math, English, and science. During this same time, Jeffs also formed a group of men known as "Helaman's Army," referencing a group of holy soldiers from their scriptures, The Book of Mormon. This group would enter members' homes and search for anything that was deemed unholy, or discouraged by the church. If anything was found, members would be disciplined accordingly. Banned items included most secular books, including children's books where animals had human characteristics, and in some cases radios, TVs, and computers. Jeffs also highly discouraged members from talking with people who were not of their faith.

This intense isolation increased Jeffs' power. Even those who no longer wanted to follow their prophet were hundreds of miles from most help, lacked education outside of Jeffs' curriculum, and had no means of supporting themselves without the church and community that had isolated them.

THE SECULAR-RELIGIOUS DIVIDE IN TURKEY

Artemis Vamianakis[†]

My people are going to learn the principles of democracy, the dictates of truth, and the teachings of science. Superstition must go. Let them worship as they will, every man can follow his own conscience provided it does not interfere with sane reason or bid him act against the liberty of his fellow men.

– Mustafa Kemal Atatürk[1]

The secularists in Turkey haven't underestimated religion they just made the mistake of believing they could control it with the power of the army alone.

– Orhan Pamuk[2]

The future, secular or religious, is *the* critical issue in Turkey. The origins of secularism date back to the Republic's first president, Mustafa Kemal Atatürk, the father of the modern secular Turkish state. Yet this secularism exists in a state where 99 percent of the population is Muslim.[3] Recently, the secular state has been challenged. The debate over a headscarf ban in universities has caused secular-religious tension. While Turkey traditionally banned the headscarf, a proposed amendment to lift the ban in Universities led to turmoil and protest. Ultimately, the amendment was overturned by the Constitutional Court, but the debate over the headscarf persists, from secular and religious alike. Additionally, in 2002, the AKP (Justice and Development), a political party said to have an Islamic platform, gained power. In 2007, the AKP's Abdullah Gül was elected President of Turkey. Gül and the AKP party continue

---

[†]   Quinney Research Fellow, S.J. Quinney College of Law, University of Utah (J.D. Candidate 2009). I would like to thank Professor Guiora for giving me the opportunity to work on this book project, and both Professor Guiora and Kevin Pendergast, for allowing me the great privilege of publishing some of my research in this Appendix—it has been an honor.

[1]   First President of the Republic of Turkey; father of the modern secular state in Turkey.

[2]   Prominent Turkish novelist and professor, winner of the 2006 Nobel Prize in Literature.

[3]   99.8 percent Muslim (mostly Sunni), other 0.2 percent mostly Christians and Jews; CIA World Factbook, Turkey, *available at* https://www.cia.gov/library/publications/the-world-factbook/geos/tu.html.

to draw strong opposition from vocal secularists concerned about the future of the modern Republic.

THE ORIGINS OF SECULARISM IN TURKEY

The secular-religious debate in Turkey dates back to the Ottoman Empire. "In the Ottoman Empire headed by the Sultan, religion played a major role in the public as well as private spheres of life. Education was primarily given by Islamic scholars in religious madrasa schools and Islamic rule of law, Sharia, was in place."[4] While Sharia law governed the Muslims, the Ottomans used what was called a "millet system" to govern religious minorities. Millet communities were organized around religious affiliation and people stayed within their millet.[5] The head of each millet community was accountable to the Sultan, but each millet had a great deal of power within its internal community. Millet communities each governed by their own law, but when any crime was committed against a Muslim, Sharia law was applied. The millet system "allowed great degree of religious, cultural and ethnic continuity to non-Muslim populations across more than three continents. At the same time it permitted their incorporation into the Ottoman administrative, economic and political system. The Ottoman-appointed governor collected taxes and provided security, while the local religious or cultural matters were left to the regional communities to decide."[6]

The millet system lost supremacy with the rise of nationalism, and the Ottomans searched for new ways to govern the vast territory of religious minorities. By the end of the 19th century, Turkey was "divided into two camps, the Islamists reformists and Westerners. Although they shared a similar goal, the modernization of Turkey, they had different views about how to reach that goal."[7] The Ottoman Empire was defeated in World War I. A young General, Mustafa Kemal, and his followers waged a Turkish revolutionary war against the Allied Forces.[8]

---

4   "Secularism: The Turkish Experience," Transcript, by Omer Baristiran, December 2004—Philadelphia, p. 4; *available at* http://www.secularisminturkey.net/docs/Secular-Transcript.pdf.

5   For example, the Greek Orthodox individuals in the Ottoman Empire stayed within the Greek Orthodox millet community.

6   *Id.*

7   *Id.* at 5.

8   *See Id.* at 5.

FREEDOM FROM RELIGION

In 1923, Turkey became an independent state and President Mustafa Kemal Atatürk[9] founded the modern secular Republic. Under Atatürk's authoritarian leadership, Turkey introduced a set of legal, social, economic, and political reforms[10] which revolutionized Turkey, turning it from a monarchy to a republic, from a theocracy to a secular state.[11] The reforms included a new constitution based on national sovereignty, a new civil code modeled after the Swiss code, and a new penal code modeled after Italy.[12] The reformed constitution annulled the article stipulating that Islam was the official religion[13] and placed democracy and secularism at the forefront; "The Republic of Turkey is a democratic, secular, and social state."[14] The principle of secularism is one of several

---

9   Mustafa Kemal was a national hero, later honored with the name "Atatürk," i.e., father of the Turks. Atatürk died in 1938, at the age of 57, after being the president for 15 years.

10   Often referred to as the "Kemal Reforms" or "Atatürk's Reforms." For a complete description of reforms, see Artun Unsal, *Atatürk's Reforms: A Realization of an Utopia by a Realist,* THE TURKISH YEARBOOK, p. 31. Paper presented to the Seminar on Nehru and Atatürk, New Delhi, November 28, 1981, *available at* http://www. politics.ankara.edu.tr/dosyalar/MMTY/19/2_by_artun_unsal.pdf.

11   Artun Unsal, *Atatürk's Reforms: A Realization of an Utopia by a Realist,* THE TURKISH YEARBOOK, p. 33. Paper presented to the Seminar on Nehru and Atatürk, New Delhi, November 28, 1981, *available at* http://www.politics.ankara.edu.tr/dosyalar/MMTY/19/2_by_artun_unsal.pdf.

12   *Id.* at 32.

13   *Id.*

14   CONSTITUTION OF THE REPUBLIC OF TURKEY Preamble, (stating "The recognition that no protection shall be accorded to an activity contrary to Turkish national interests, the principle of the indivisibility of the existence of Turkey with its state and territory, **Turkish historical and moral values or the nationalism, principles, reforms and modernism of Atatürk and that, as required by the principle of secularism**, there shall be no interference whatsoever by sacred religious feelings in state affairs and politics; the acknowledgment that it is the birthright of every Turkish citizen to lead an honourable life and to develop his or her material and spiritual assets under the aegis of national culture, civilization and the rule of law, through the exercise of the fundamental rights and freedoms set forth in this Constitution in conformity with the requirements of equality and social justice") (emphasis added).

See also, CONSTITUTION OF THE REPUBLIC OF TURKEY, Article 2 (stating "**The Republic of Turkey is a democratic, secular and social state governed** by the rule of law; bearing in mind the concepts of public peace, national solidarity and justice; respecting human rights; loyal to the nationalism of Atatürk, and based on the fundamental tenets set forth in the Preamble.") (emphasis added).

irrevocable parts of the constitution.[15] Atatürk also utilized the military to act as the guardian of the secular state; the Turkish Armed Forces (TSK) continues to play the guardian role in politics today.[16]

RELIGIOUS FREEDOM

The interplay between religion and the secular state in Turkey is a complicated one. The Turkish Constitution provides for freedom of religion and freedom of religious practice.[17] However, that freedom can be constitutionally curtailed under color of law if it is found to threaten the secular state.[18] In practice, the Turkish government generally respects religious freedom, "however, the Government imposes limitations on Islamic and other religious groups and significant restrictions on Islamic

---

15   Under CONSTITUTION OF THE REPUBLIC OF TURKEY, Article 4, certain provisions established under the previous articles are irrevocable including the following principles: The Turkish State is a Republic; The Republic of Turkey is a democratic, secular, and social state governed by the rule of law; The Turkish state, with its territory and nation, is an indivisible entity. Its language is Turkish; its flag, the form of which is prescribed by the relevant law, is composed of a white crescent and a star on a red background; its national anthem is the "Independence March;" and its capital is Ankara.

16   CIA World Factbook, Turkey, *available at* https://www.cia.gov/library/publications/the-world-factbook/geos/tu.html.

17   *See* CONSTITUTION REPUBLIC OF TURKEY, Article 24: "Everyone has the right to freedom of conscience, religious belief and conviction. Acts of worship, religious services, and ceremonies shall be conducted freely, provided that they do not violate the provisions of Article 14. No one shall be compelled to worship, or to participate in religious ceremonies and rites, to reveal religious beliefs and convictions, or be blamed or accused because of his religious beliefs and convictions. Education and instruction in religion and ethics shall be conducted under state supervision and control. Instruction in religious culture and moral education shall be compulsory in the curricula of primary and secondary schools. Other religious education and instruction shall be subject to the individual's own desire, and in the case of minors, to the request of their legal representatives. No one shall be allowed to exploit or abuse religion or religious feelings, or things held sacred by religion, in any manner whatsoever, for the purpose of personal or political influence, or for even partially basing the fundamental, social, economic, political, and legal order of the state on religious tenets."

18   *See* CONSTITUTION REPUBLIC OF TURKEY, Article 14: "None of the rights and freedoms embodied in the Constitution shall be exercised with the aim of violating the indivisible integrity of the state with its territory and nation, and endangering the existence of the democratic and secular order of the Turkish Republic based upon human rights."

religious expression in government offices and state-run institutions, including universities, for the stated reason of preserving the 'secular state.'"[19] "Secularists in the military, judiciary, and other branches of the bureaucracy continued to wage campaigns against what they label as Islamic fundamentalism. These groups view religious fundamentalism as a threat to the secular state. The National Security Council and Turkish General Staff categorize religious fundamentalism as a threat to public safety."[20]

While the majority of Turks are Muslim, religious minorities play a significant role in the complex secular-religious debate. In 2008, the United States Department of State reported that:

> Religious minorities said they were effectively blocked from careers in state institutions because of their faith. Minority religious groups also faced difficulties in worshipping, registering with the Government, and training their followers. Although religious speech and persuasion is legal, some Muslims, Christians, and Baha'is faced a few restrictions and occasional harassment for alleged proselytizing or holding unauthorized meetings.

> There were reports of societal abuses and discrimination based on religious affiliation, belief, or practice. Violent attacks and continued threats against non-Muslims during the reporting period created an atmosphere of pressure and diminished freedom for some non-Muslim communities. Many Christians, Baha'is, and Muslims faced societal suspicion and mistrust, and more-radical Islamist elements continued to express anti-Semitic sentiments. Additionally, persons wishing to convert from Islam sometimes experienced social harassment and violence from relatives and neighbors.[21]

According to the Turkish government, 99 percent of the population is Muslim, largely Sunni.[22] After the Treaty of Lusanne[23] in 1923, Turkey

---

19   *International Religious Freedom Report, Turkey*, U.S. DEPARTMENT OF STATE, 2008, *available at* http://www.state.gov/g/drl/rls/irf/2008/108476.htm.

20   *Id.*

21   *International Religious Freedom Report, Turkey*, U.S. DEPARTMENT OF STATE, 2008, *available at* http://www.state.gov/g/drl/rls/irf/2008/108476.htm.

22   The U.S. State Department reports that "[a]ccording to the human rights non-governmental organization (NGO) Mazlum-Der and representatives of various religious minority communities, the actual percentage of Muslims is slightly lower. *Id.*

23   Peace Treaty signed following the Turkish War for Independence.

officially recognized three minority religious groups: Greek Orthodox Christians, Armenian Orthodox Christians, and Jews.[24] "The Government interpreted the 1923 Lausanne Treaty as granting special legal minority status exclusively to these three recognized groups, although the treaty text refers broadly to 'non-Muslim minorities' without listing specific groups. This recognition does not extend to the religious leadership organs," however, which causes a great deal of tension.[25] "For example, the Ecumenical (Greek Orthodox) and Armenian Patriarchates continued to seek legal recognition of their status as patriarchates rather than foundations, the absence of which prevents them from having the right to own and transfer property and train religious clergy."[26]

The Turkish government also faces international political pressure to improve religious freedom and minority rights. For example, in his first trip to Turkey, President Barack Obama of the United States urged Turkey to open the Halki Seminary, the seat of the Greek Orthodox Patriarchate, Bartholomew.[27]

> "For democracies cannot be static—they must move forward. Freedom of religion and expression lead to a strong and vibrant civil society that only strengthens the state, which is why steps like reopening the Halki Seminary will send such an important signal inside Turkey and beyond. An enduring commitment to the rule of law is the only way to achieve the security that comes from justice for all people. Robust minority rights let societies benefit from the full measure of contributions from all citizens."[28]

SECULAR-RELIGIOUS TENSION

While religious freedom remains a heated issue among religious and secular Muslims and religious minorities, Turkey's secular policies have also faced significant pressure on other fronts. For example, presently,

---

24   *International Religious Freedom Report, Turkey*, U.S. DEPARTMENT OF STATE, 2008, *available at* http://www.state.gov/g/drl/rls/irf/2008/108476.htm; in 2008— approximately 65,000 Armenian Orthodox Christians, 23,000 Jews and up to 4,000 Greek Orthodox Christians.

25   *Id.*

26   *Id.*

27   Sedat Ergin, *An Inventory of Obama's Visit*, TURKISH DAILY NEWS, April 9, 2009.

28   President of the United States, Barack Obama, speech to Turkish Parliament, April 2009, *available at* http://arama.hurriyet.com.tr/arsivnews.aspx?id=11376661.

Turkey is seeking to become a part of the European Union, however this bid has placed Turkey in the spotlight for reform. According to the EU Council of Ministers, Turkey must "strengthen legal and constitutional guarantees for the right to freedom of expression in line with Article 10 of the European Convention of Human Rights [and] address in that context the situation of those persons in prison sentenced for expressing non-violent opinions."[29] Furthermore, Turkey must "guarantee full enjoyment by all individuals without any discrimination and irrespective of their language, race, colour, sex, political opinion, philosophical belief or religion of all human rights and fundamental freedoms [and] further develop conditions for the enjoyment of freedom of thought, conscience and religion."[30] While the EU requires this action, Turkish secularists fear that these reforms impede the secular state.

Additionally, the secular-religious debate gained recent tension over the headscarf ban and the AKP's rise to power.

THE HEADSCARF DEBATE

The debate over the headscarf[31] truly brings the complex secular-religious tension to light. Turkey has traditionally banned wearing head-scarves in the public sector. Specifically, women who wear headscarves are banned from higher education, working in positions such as teachers, lawyers, and parliamentarians.[32] In 2006, the ban expanded to cover non-state institutions; women lawyers and journalists who refused to comply with the ban were expelled from public buildings including universities and courtrooms.[33]

---

29 CONSTITUTIONAL IMPLICATIONS FOR ACCESSION TO THE EUROPEAN UNION, European Commission for Democracy through Law (Council of Europe Publishing) (2002), p. 65 (quoting from the report of the Council of Ministers).

30 CONSTITUTIONAL IMPLICATIONS FOR ACCESSION TO THE EUROPEAN UNION, European Commission for Democracy through Law (Council of Europe Publishing) (2002), p. 66 (quoting from the report of the Council of Ministers).

31 "Headscarf" refers to the covering of a woman's hair by a piece of cloth, part of the traditional hijab (head cover and modest dress).

32 *Turkey: Situation of Women who Wear Headscarves*, THE UN REFUGEE AGENCY, May 20, 2008, *available at* http://www.unhcr.org/refworld/country,,IRBC,, TUR,,4885a91a8,0.html.

33 *Id.*

In 1998, the headscarf ban was challenged in the European Court of Human Rights.[34] Leyla Sahin, a medical student at Istanbul University who was refused access to an exam, and later refused enrollment in a course because she was wearing a headscarf, brought a case challenging the ban. Sahin argued that the ban violated her right to an education and also was active discrimination. The Court rejected her appeal, holding that there had been no violation of the following provisions of the European Convention on Human Rights:

Article 9—freedom of thought, conscience, and religion;

Article 2 of Protocol No. 1—right to education;

Article 8—right to respect for private and family rights;

Article 10—freedom of expression; and

Article 14—prohibition of discrimination.[35]

The court ruled that the headscarf ban, based on the principles of secularism and equality "was justified to maintain order and avoid giving preference to any religion."[36] Further the "court did not lose sight of the fact that there were extremist political movements in Turkey which sought to impose on society as a whole their religious symbols and conception of a society founded on religious precepts."[37]

While those opposed to the ban found the *Sahin* case to be a resounding defeat, the debate continued. In 2008, a survey of approximately 1,500 students in 26 universities in Turkey revealed that 52 percent were against the headscarf ban but 35 percent believed that lifting the ban would "increase social pressure against students who do not wear a headscarf."[38] The Christian Science Monitor reported that "many young women who

---

34   *Sahin v. Turkey*, European Court of Human Rights, Application no. 44774/98.

35   *See* Grand Chamber Judgment, *Leyla Sahin v. Turkey*, Press release issued by the Registrar, *available at* http://www.echr.coe.int/Eng/Press/2005/Nov/Grand ChamberJudgmentLeylaSahinvTurkey101105.htm.

36   *Court Backs Turkish Headscarf Ban* BBC, November 10, 2005, *available at* http://news.bbc.co.uk/2/hi/europe/4424776.stm.

37   *Id.*

38   Grand Chamber Judgement, *Leyla Sahin v. Turkey*, Press release issued by the Registrar, *available at* http://www.echr.coe.int/Eng/Press/2005/Nov/Grand ChamberJudgmentLeylaSahinvTurkey101105.htm (citing the *Turkish Daily News*, March 24, 2008).

wear headscarves ... moved abroad in order to complete their university studies" while others "choose to wear a wig covering their headscarves so that they can attend university classes in Turkey."[39]

In February 2008, the Turkish Parliament, headed by the efforts of the AKP, approved a constitutional amendment designed to lift the headscarf ban in universities. The amendment however was met with fervent protest from secularists. "We say it will damage secularity ... Once you do that—we believe you damage democracy."[40] In anticipation of the amendment, thousands of people rallied in Ankara against the amendment. "'Turkey is secular and will remain secular,' shouted protesters as they waved national flags and banners of Mustafa Kemal Ataturk."[41] One protestor noted, "I am a true believer in Islam, but my religion is in my heart, not in what I wear. I feel that the headscarf will bring the country backwards.... Turkey is unique in this region. It has modernized Islam and we should be leading other Muslim countries."[42]

On February 27, 2008, Turkey's opposition party filed an appeal with the Turkish Constitutional Court to overturn the amendment. Ultimately, on June 5, 2008, the Constitutional Court annulled the proposed amendment to lift the headscarf ban, calling the amendment a violation of the nature of the secular state, ruling that the amendment was therefore unconstitutional.[43] The court decision re-imposed the headscarf ban on university campuses. Does banning a headscarf unnecessarily infringe on individual rights, or is it vital to the preservation of the secular Republic? Either way, for now, the ban remains in place and Turkish women face a

---

39 Grand Chamber Judgement, *Leyla Sahin v. Turkey*, Press release issued by the Registrar, *available at* http://www.echr.coe.int/Eng/Press/2005/Nov/Grand ChamberJudgmentLeylaSahinvTurkey101105.htm (citing Christian Science Monitor, February 11, 2008).

40 Ural Akbulut, Rector of Middle East Technical University, cited in *Turkey Eases Ban on Headscarves*, BBC, February 9, 2008, *available at* http://news.bbc.co.uk/2/hi/europe/7236128.stm.

41 Paul de Bendern, *Secular Turks Rally Against Muslim Headscarf Reform*, REUTERS, February 2, 2008, *available at* http://www.reuters.com/article/newsMaps/idUSL0221636420080202.

42 Fatma Sarikaya, retired engineer, quoted in Paul de Bendern, *Secular Turks Rally Against Muslim Headscarf Reform*, REUTERS, February 2, 2008, *available at* http://www.reuters.com/article/newsMaps/idUSL0221636420080202.

43 *See International Religious Freedom Report, Turkey*, U.S. DEPARTMENT OF STATE, 2008, *available at* http://www.state.gov/g/drl/rls/irf/2008/108476.htm.

hopeless dilemma, to either express their religious beliefs or take part in the public sphere.

AKP—JUSTICE AND DEVELOPMENT PARTY

Another recent source of secular-religious tension is the rise of the Justice and Development Party (Adalet ve Kalkünma Partisi, referred to as the "AKP") to power. The AKP was formed by politicians with roots in the Islamic movement. In 2002, the AKP gained several seats in Parliament gaining significant power. The AKP gained even more power after the general election in 2007. In the Turkish general election for members of the Grand National Assembly, Turkish parliament, the Justice and Development Party led the vote, winning 16,327,291 votes (46.6 percent), 341 seats.[44] In a controversial election, the Grand National Assembly elected Abdulla Gül, a member of the Islamist-oriented Justice and Development Party (AKP) as Turkey's 11th president on August 28, 2007.

> The nomination of Gül—whose wife wears a headscarf—to the Turkish presidency last year provoked a parliamentary boycott by opposition lawmakers and mass demonstrations by secularists, as well as prompting Turkish army chiefs to warn that they would act to protect secularism if necessary. In response, Edrogan called snap elections with AKP returning to government with a landslide 46.6 percent share of the vote. Gül was re-nominated to the presidency and elected by parliamentary vote the following month.

On March 14, 2008, the chief prosecutor, Abdurrahman Yalcinkaya, filed a closure case in the Constitutional Court against the AKP, asking the court to shut down the party and ban its members from elected office for five years.[45] The prosecutor accused the party "of spearheading 'anti-secular activities' in violation of the Turkish constitution."[46] "While the prosecutor acknowledged that the AKP's program and its written statutes were not unconstitutional, the indictment charged that AKP

---

44   *Turkey's Parliamentary Election*, GLOBAL ECONOMY MATTERS, *available at* http:// globaleconomydoesmatter.blogspot.com/2007/07/turkeys-early-parliamentary-election-of.html, last visited July 8, 2008.

45   Soner Cagaptay, *Will the Turkish Constitutional Court Ban the AKP?* THE WASHINGTON INSTITUTE FOR NEAR EAST POLICY, Policy watch #1355, March 19, 2008, *available at* http://www.washingtoninstitute.org/print.php?template= C05&CID=2731.

46   *Id.*

had 'in actions and verbal statements acted against laws and the Constitution.'"[47]

Ultimately, following days of deliberation, the court voted against indictment. The court chose to impose a financial penalty which stripped the party of half of its funding for the following year.[48] The court also issued a "'serious warning' [to the AKP] that it was steering the country in too Islamic a direction. Legislation pressed by the party that would have allowed women in head scarves to attend universities, for example, raised suspicions about its agenda."[49] The AKP and its supporters breathed a sigh of relief; "this verdict means a very important milestone has been passed . . . It has been very tense—the uncertainty involved in all this has been very troubling. We couldn't plan for anything. There's now great relief that the uncertainty has gone."[50] The opposition, however, said that the "court's verdict failed to solve the country's political crisis."[51] Nationalist Party leader Devlet Bahceli, warned that "Premier Erdogan and AKP should see that having problems with the constitutional order and the foundation principles of the state can jeopardize the democratic regime."[52]

TURKEY'S FUTURE—SECULAR OR RELIGIOUS?

What is the future of Turkey—continued secularism under the tradition of Atatürk, Islamization under the leadership of the AKP, or can the two

---

47   *Turkey: International Religious Freedom Report, 2008*, Bureau of Democracy, Human Rights and Labor, Department of the State, September 19, 2008, *available at* http://www.state.gov/g/drl/rls/irf/2008/108476.htm (last visited October 6, 2008).

48   *See* Simon Hooper, *Relief in Turkey over Court Verdict*, CNN, August 5, 2008, *available at* http://www.cnn.com/2008/WORLD/europe/07/31/turkey.reaction/index.html?eref=rss_topstories.

49   Sabrina Tavernise, *Turkish Court Calls Ruling Party Constitutional*, NEW YORK TIMES, July 31, 2008.

50   AKP's Deputy Chairman of External Affairs, Suat Kiniklioglu, quoted in Simon Hooper, *Relief in Turkey over Court Verdict*, CNN, August 5, 2008, *available at* http://www.cnn.com/2008/WORLD/europe/07/31/turkey.reaction/index.html?eref=rss_topstories.

51   Simon Hooper, *Relief in Turkey over Court Verdict*, CNN, August 5, 2008, *available at* http://www.cnn.com/2008/WORLD/europe/07/31/turkey.reaction/index.html?eref=rss_topstories.

52   *Id.*

somehow work in tandem? Speaking on secularism, Prime Minister Edrogan said "the secularism principle of the country should be seen as a tool to unite society not to divide it. . . . I believe we have a great task as a nation. This is to convey secularism to the next generations by cherishing it not as a discriminating but as a unifying principle."[53] President Gül noted that the "task of a democratic and secular state is to give the chance to everybody to practice their beliefs freely and give the chance to those without religious beliefs to live without facing any oppression."[54]

How will Turkey balance religious freedom against the interests of the secular state? While the future is unclear, what is clear is that based on recent examples of the headscarf and AKP party, the tension and fervent debate is far from over.

---

53   *Secularism Should Unite, Not Divide Society: Erodoethan*, TURKISH DAILY NEWS, February 6, 2009.

54   *Id.*

INDEX

Absolutist regimes and religious
    extremism, 15–16
Adams, Brooke, 98n12
American media coverage of FLDS
    church, 80–83
Amir, Yigal, 11, 33, 77
Applegate, Marshall, 99n21
Arafat, Yaser, 32
Assembly. *See* Freedom of association
Association. *See* Freedom of association
Atatürk, Mustafa Kemal, 25
Atran, Scott, 62n9

Ballin, Dr. Hirsch, 121, 123
Barr, Daniel C., 73n4
Bawer, Bruce, 4n8
Ben-Gurion, Prime Minister David, 86n2
Ben-Yair, Michael, 35, 37
Black, Justice Hugo, 31
Bouyeri, Mohammed, 22, 47, 121
Boyer, Pascal, 11
Bozkurt, Göksel, 51–52n77
Brandeis, Justice Louis, 31
Brandenburg v. Ohio, 39–40
    expanding *Brandenburg*, 120
    intermediate or strict scrutiny, 44–45
    lowering intent element, 42–43
    unprotected speech, 40–42
Britain. *See* United Kingdom
Brown, Gordon, 3
Brownfeld, Allan C., 34n21–22,
    34n24, 36n31
Bustillo, Miguel, 101n26

Cantwell v. Connecticut, 44, 60n5
Cartner, Holly, 25n33
Chaplinsky v. New Hampshire, 40
Chemerinsky, Erwin, 67n27, 68n28
Chertoff, Michael, 53n88
Church and state separation
    Israel, 87–91
    permanency of the state, 85–87

Church and state separation (*cont.*)
    state and religious extremists in
      Israel, 91–93
    U.S. First Amendment, 85
Churchill, Winston, 1
Clinton, President Bill, 32
Cliteur, Paul, 21
Cultural considerations and religious liberty
    female genital cutting, 107–109
    headscarves, 18, 24–25, 101–106,
      122–123
    honor killings, 109–111, 114–115, 123–124
Cumper, Peter, 53n83

Dawkins, Richard, 52
Dayan, Moshe, 32n13
Dennis et al. v. U.S., 31n8
Din rodef, 34
Dismantling Gaza settlements, 18–19
Dismantling settlements, proposed, 32–33
Docherty, Neil, 47n61
Doctrine of certitude, 16
Dome of the Rock, 78–79
Doughty, Steve, 2n2
Dvir, Rabbi Shmuel, 34

ECHR (European Convention on Human
    Rights), 20–21, 38, 56
Employment Div., Dept. of Human Resources of
    State of Oregon v. Smith, 20
Eskin, Avigdor, 34–35
European Convention on Human Rights
    (ECHR), 20–21, 38, 56
European Court on Human
    Rights, 38, 103
Extremist religion. *See* Religious extremism

Fattah, Geoffrey, 101n25
Fatwas, 23, 124
Female genital cutting (FCG), 107–109
Firestone, Rueven, 12n2

FREEDOM FROM RELIGION